PARSIFAL

The idea of a music drama based on the legend of Parsifal and the knights of the Holy Grail occured to Richard Wagner as early as 1846, when he was working on *Lohengrin*, the score that launched his career as the leading German opera composer of the Nineteenth Century. The Swan Knight Lohengrin is in fact the son of Parsifal, and during his farewell aria to his bride, Elsa, he describes the temple of the Grail at Monsalvat. Wagner completed *Parsifal*, his last work, in 1882. It is considered by many to be the ultimate development of the composer's lifelong struggle to mate text, music and action into an indivisible whole, the *Gesamtkunstwerk*. Because of the music drama's sacred nature, it is held by many to be much more than a mere theatrical entertainment.

The primary source for *Parsifal*, which he termed a *Bühnenweihfestspiel* (stage-consecrational-festival-play), came from the epic medieval poem *Parzival* by Wolfram von Eschenbach (1170-1220), who appears as a character in the composer's *Tannhäuser*. It is thought that Eschenbach took his material from the *Legends of the Grail* (1180) by the French trouvere Chrétien de Troyes. Although *Parsifal* embodies both Buddist and Christian doctrine, its basic message remains universal: enlightenment through compassion brings salvation. This theme stands in contrast to such earlier Wagner works as *Der Fliegende Holländer*, *Tannhäuser* and *Tristan und Isolde* in which salvation is gained through a selfless woman's love.

Wagner ordained that *Parsifal* be staged only in Bayreuth, at his own theater; only here, he felt, could a proper production of the work be insured. The music drama was first seen there on July 26, 1882, six months before the composer's death. In spite of Wagner's wishes, Heinrich Conried decided to present the work during his first season as general manager of the Metropolitan Opera in 1903. Protests raged on both sides of the Atlantic, and Wagner's widow Cosima brought the issue to court. Ultimately Conried won his battle and the Metropolitan's version — conducted by Alfred Hertz and starring Milka Ternina, Alois Burgstaller and Anton Van Rooy as Kundry, Parsifal and Amfortas — was hailed by the critics as superior to Bayreuth's. After this, *Parsifal* entered the repertory of many other theaters, and despite its extreme length and philosophical nature, is seldom absent from the boards. In New York, at the Metropolitan, it has become a traditional part of the Easter season.

G. SCHIRMER'S
COLLECTION OF
OPERA LIBRETTOS

PARSIFAL

Music Drama in Three Acts

by

Richard Wagner

English Version by
STEWART ROBB

Ed. 2632

G. SCHIRMER, *Inc.*

Important Notice

Performances of this opera must be licensed by the publisher.

All rights of any kind with respect to this opera and any parts thereof, including but not limited to stage, radio, television, motion picture, mechanical reproduction, translation, printing, and selling are strictly reserved.

License to perform this work, in whole or in part, whether with instrumental or keyboard accompaniment, must be secured in writing from the Publisher. Terms will be quoted upon request.

Copying of either separate parts or the whole of this work, by hand or by any other process, is unlawful and punishable under the provisions of the U.S.A. Copyright Act.

The use of any copies, including arrangements and orchestrations, other than those issued by the Publisher, is forbidden.

All inquiries should be directed to the Publisher:

G. Schirmer Rental Department
445 Bellvale Road
Chester, NY 10918
(914) 469-2271

45903c

THE STORY

ACT I. Gurnemanz, knight of the brotherhood of the Holy Grail, rises from sleep with his two young esquires in a forest near the castle of Monsalvat in the Spanish Pyrenees. Two other knights arrive to prepare a morning bath for the ailing monarch, Amfortas, who has an incurable wound. They are interrupted by Kundry, an ageless woman of many guises, who rushes in wildly with balsam for Amfortas. The king and his suite now enter, accept the gift and proceed to the nearby lake. Gurnemanz tells his companions how a beautiful woman betrayed Amfortas into the hands of Klingsor, a sorcerer who, when denied admittance to the brotherhood, was able to seize the sacred spear from the king and inflict upon him a wound that can be healed only by a guileless fool. Suddenly a swan falls to the ground, an arrow in its breast. The knights drag in a youth, Parsifal, whom Gurnemanz gently rebukes for his foolhardy act. The boy flings away his bow and arrows in shame but cannot explain his conduct or even state his name. Kundry arises to tell the youth's history: his father Gamuret died in battle; his mother Herzeleide reared the boy in the forest, but now she too is dead. As Kundry falls in a trance, the knights carry Amfortas' litter back from the lake. Gurnemanz leads Parsifal away to the castle of the Grail, hoping the youth may be the guileless fool.

In the lofty Hall of the Grail, Amfortas is surrounded by his knights, who prepare for the ritual of the Lord's Supper. The voice of the king's father, the aged Titurel, bids him uncover the holy vessel and proceed, but Amfortas at first hesitates, his anguish rising in the presence of the blood of Christ. At length Titurel orders the esquires to uncover the chalice, which casts its glow about the hall. As the bread and wine are offered, an invisible choir is heard from the height of the dome. Parsifal, who has remained mute through the ceremonies, understands nothing — but when Amfortas cries out in pain he clutches his heart. Although Gurnemanz angrily drives the boy away, a voice reiterates the prophecy.

ACT II. Seated in his dark tower, Klingsor summons Kundry to seduce Parsifal; having secured the spear through Amfortas' weakness, he now wishes to inherit the Grail. Kundry, who hopes for redemption, protests in vain.

The scene changes to a magic garden, where Parsifal is surrounded by Flower Maidens who beg for his embrace. He resists them and they disappear. In their place is Kundry, transformed into a beautiful siren, who woos him with tender memories of his childhood and mother. As she breaks down his resistance and offers a passionate kiss, the youth recoils; at last he understands the mystery of Amfortas' wound and his own mission. Kundry now tries to lure him through pity for the weary life she has led ever since she laughed at Christ on the Cross, but again she is repulsed. In desperation she calls on Klingsor for help. The magician appears on the rampart and hurls the sacred spear at Parsifal, who catches it and makes the sign of the cross. The castle falls into ruins. "You will know where to find me," Parsifal tells Kundry.

ACT III. Gurnemanz, now a hermit and grown very old, finds the penitent Kundry lifeless and exhausted in a thicket near his little hut. As he revives her, a strange knight in full armor approaches across the sunny meadow. Gurnemanz recognizes Parsifal and hails his sacred spear, whereupon the knight describes his weary wanderings in search of Amfortas and the Grail. Gurnemanz removes Parsifal's armor; Kundry washes his feet. In return he baptizes her, then exclaims at the beauty of the spring fields. The hermit replies that this is the spell of Good Friday. The tolling of distant bells announces the funeral of Titurel. Solemnly they walk to the castle.

The communion table has vanished from the Hall of the Grail. No longer able to uncover the chalice, Amfortas begs the knights to end his anguish with death. But a new leader is at hand. Parsifal touches Amfortas' breast with the sacred lance and heals the wound. Raising the sacred cup aloft, he accepts the homage of the knights as their new king. Kundry falls, dying. The brotherhood has been redeemed.

Courtesy of Opera News

CAST OF CHARACTERS

GURNEMANZ . . . . *Bass*

KUNDRY . . . . *Soprano*

AMFORTAS . . . . *Baritone*

PARSIFAL . . . . *Tenor*

TITUREL . . . . *Bass*

KLINGSOR . . . . *Bass*

FIRST KNIGHT . . . . *Tenor*

SECOND KNIGHT . . . . *Baritone*

FIRST ESQUIRE . . . . *Soprano*

SECOND ESQUIRE . . . . *Mezzo-soprano*

THIRD ESQUIRE . . . . *Tenor*

FOURTH ESQUIRE . . . . *Tenor*

A VOICE . . . . *Mezzo-soprano*

Flower Maidens, Brotherhood of the Knights, Esquires and Boys.

SYNOPSIS OF SCENES

PARSIFAL

ERSTER AUFZUG

WALD, SCHATTIG UND ERNST, DOCH
NICHT DUSTER.

*Felsiger Boden. Eine Lichtung in der
Mitte. Links aufsteigend wird der
Weg zur Gralsburg angenommen.
Der Mitte des Hintergrundes zu
senkt sich der Boden zu einem tiefer
gelegenen Waldsee hinab.—Tagesan-
bruch.—Gurnemanz und zwei Knappen sind schlafend unter einem
Baume gelagert.—Wie von der Gralsburg her, ertönt der feierliche Mor-
genweckruf der Posaunen.*

GURNEMANZ

*(erwachend und die Knappen rüt-
telnd)*

He! Ho! Waldhüter ihr!
Schlafhüter mitsammen!
So wacht doch mindest am Morgen!

*(Die beiden Knappen springen auf,
und senken sich, beschämt, sogleich
wieder auf die Knie.)*

Hört ihr den Ruf? Nun danket Gott,
dass ihr berufen ihn zu hören!

*(Er senkt sich zu ihnen ebenfalls nie-
der; gemeinschaftlich verrichten sie
stumm ihr Morgengebet; sobald die
Posaunen schweigen, erheben sie sich
dann.)*

Jetzt auf, ihr Knaben; seht nach dem
Bad.
Zeit ist's, des König's dort zu harren.
Dem Siechbett, das ihn trägt, voraus
seh' ich die Boten schon uns nah'n.

(Zwei Ritter treten auf.)

Heil euch! Wie geht's Amfortas heut?
Wohl früh verlangt er nach dem Bade:
das Heilkraut, das Gawan
mit List und Kühnheit ihm gewann,
ich wähne, dass es Lind'rung schuf?

DER ERSTE RITTER

Das wähnest du, der doch alles weiss?
Ihm kehrten sehrender nur
die Schmerzen bald zurück:
schlaflos von starkem Bresten
befahl er eifrig uns das Bad.

GURNEMANZ

Toren wir, auf Lind'rung da zu hoffen,
wo einzig Heilung lindert!
Nach allen Kräutern, allen Tränken
forscht und jagt weit durch die Welt:
ihm hilft nur eines,
nur der Eine.

ERSTER RITTER

So nenn' uns den!

GURNEMANZ

Sorgt für das Bad.

DER ERSTE KNAPPE

Seht dort, die wilde Reiterin!

ZWEITER KNAPPE

Hei!
Wie fliegen der Teufelsmähre die
Mähnen!

ERSTER RITTER

Ha! Kundry dort?

ZWEITER RITTER

Die bringt wohl wicht'ge Kunde?

ERSTER KNAPPE

Die Mähre taumelt.

ZWEITER KNAPPE

Flog sie durch die Luft?

ERSTER KNAPPE

Jetzt kriecht sie am Boden hin.

ZWEITER KNAPPE

Mit den Mähnen fegt sie das Moos.

ERSTER RITTER

Da schwingt sich die Wilde herab.

*(Kundry stürzt hastig, fast taumelnd
herein. Wilde Kleidung, hoch ge-
schürzt; Gürtel von Schlangenhäuten
lang herabhängend; schwarzes, in
losen Zöpfen flatterndes Haar; tief
braun-rötliche Gesichtsfarbe, stech-
ende schwarze Augen, zuweilen wild
aufblitzend, öfters wie todesstarr und
unbeweglich.—Sie eilt auf Gurnemanz zu und dringt ihm ein kleines
Krystallgefäss auf.)*

1

PARSIFAL

ACT I

The domain of the Grail. A shadowy forest, impressive, but not gloomy. A glade in the middle. A road leading to the Grail's castle rises left. In the background can be glimpsed a low-lying forest lake. Daybreak. Two young squires are lying asleep under a tree. Gurnemanz, an old but vigorous man, also under the tree, has just awakened, for the solemn morning reveille of trombones is heard at rise of curtain.

GURNEMANZ

(shaking the youngsters)

Hey! Ho! Woodkeepers there!
Sleepkeepers more likely!
Awake at least with the morning!

(The two squires spring up.)

There is the call. Give thanks to God
that you are privileged to hear it!

(He sinks to his knees with the squires and they offer up a silent morning prayer, then they rise slowly.)

Now up, young fellows; see to the bath!
Time now to wait there for your master.

(He looks off, left.)

The sickbed bearing him is near:
I see the heralds coming now.

(Two heralds appear.)

Hail there! How fares the King today?
He seeks his healing bath quite early.
The balsam which Gawain
with skill and boldness won for him—
I trust it helped to ease his pain?

FIRST KNIGHT

You only trust, you who know the truth?
Amfortas' pains soon returned,
and keener than before.
Sleepless, from sheer exhaustion,
he urged us get the bath prepared.

GURNEMANZ

(drooping his head sorrowfully)

Fools are we, to hope to ease his torment,
where only healing eases!
For every simple, every potion,
seek and hunt throughout the world.
There's but one healing,
but one Healer!

FIRST KNIGHT

Then give his name!

GURNEMANZ

Look to the bath!

FIRST SQUIRE

See there! The woman riding wild!

SECOND SQUIRE

Hey!
The mane of her devil's mare is flying!

FIRST KNIGHT

Ha! Kundry there?

SECOND KNIGHT

No doubt with weighty tidings.

FIRST SQUIRE

The mare is reeling.

SECOND SQUIRE

Did she fly through air?

FIRST SQUIRE

She's skimming along the ground.

SECOND SQUIRE

And her mane is sweeping the moss.

FIRST KNIGHT

The wild woman flings from her horse.
(Kundry rushes in, almost reeling; wild garb fastened high; girdle of snake-skin hanging; long, black hair flowing in loose locks; dark brownish-red complexion, piercing black eyes, sometimes wild and blazing, but usually fixed and glassy. She hurries over to Gurnemanz and presses upon him a small crystal flask.)

1

KUNDRY

Hier! Nimm du! Balsam . . .

GURNEMANZ

Woher brachtest du dies?

KUNDRY

Von weiter her, als du denken kannst:
hilft der Balsam nicht,
Arabian birgt dann
nichts mehr zu seinem Heil.
Fragt nicht weiter! Ich bin müde.
(*Sie wirft sich auf den Boden.*)
(*Ein Zug von Knappen und Rittern,
die Sänfte tragend und geleitend, in
welcher Amfortas ausgestreckt liegt,
gelangt auf die Bühne.*)

GURNEMANZ

Er naht, sie bringen ihn getragen.
Oh weh'! Wie trag' ich's im Gemüte,
in seiner Mannheit stolzer Blüte
des siegreichsten Geschlechtes Herrn
als seines Siechtums Knecht zu seh'n!
(*zu den Knappen*)
Behutsam! Hört, der König stöhnt.
(*Jene stellen das Siechbett nieder.*)

AMFORTAS

(*erhebt sich ein wenig*)
Recht so! Habt Dank! Ein wenig Rast.
Nach wilder Schmerzensnacht
nun Waldes Morgenpracht!
Im heil'gen See
wohl labt mich auch die Welle:
es staunt das Weh',
die Schmerzensnacht wird helle.
Gawan!

ERSTER RITTER

Herr, Gawan weilte nicht
Da seines Heilkraut's Kraft,
wie schwer er's auch errungen,
doch deine Hoffnung trog,
hat er auf neue Sucht sich fortge-
schwungen.

AMFORTAS

Ohn' Urlaub? Möge das er sühnen,
dass schlecht er Gralsgebote hält!
O wehe ihm, dem trotzig Kühnen,
wenn er in Klingsor's Schlingen fällt!
So breche Keiner mir den Frieden!
Ich harre dess', der mir beschieden:
"durch Mitleid wissend"
war's nicht so?

GURNEMANZ

Uns sagtest du es so.

AMFORTAS

"der reine Tor."
Mich dünkt ihn zu erkennen:
dürft' ich den Tod ihn nennen!

GURNEMANZ

Doch zuvor: versuch' es noch mit
diesem!
(*Er reicht ihm das Fläschchen.*)

AMFORTAS

Woher dies heimliche Gefäss?

GURNEMANZ

Dir ward es aus Arabia hergeführt.

AMFORTAS

Und wer gewann es?

GURNEMANZ

Dort liegt's, das wilde Weib.
Auf, Kundry! Komm!
(*Sie weigert sich.*)

AMFORTAS

Du, Kundry?
Muss ich dir nochmals danken,
du rastlos scheue Magd?
Wohlan, den Balsam nun versuch' ich
noch;
es sei aus Dank für deine Treue.

KUNDRY

(*unruhig am Boden liegend*)
Nicht Dank! Ha ha! Was wird es
helfen!
Nicht Dank! Fort, fort in's Bad!
(*Amfortas gibt das Zeichen zum Aufbruch; der Zug entfernt sich nach
dem tieferen Hintergrunde zu. —
Gurnemanz, schwermütig nachblickend, und Kundry fortwährend auf
dem Boden gelagert, sind zurück-
geblieben. Knappen gehen ab und
zu.*)

DRITTER KNAPPE

He! Du da!
Was liegst du dort wie ein wildes Tier?

KUNDRY

Sind die Tiere hier nicht heilig?

DRITTER KNAPPE

Ja! doch ob heilig du,
das wissen wir grad' noch nicht.

KUNDRY

Take this! Balsam!

GURNEMANZ

But where did you get it?

KUNDRY

From farther off than your thoughts
can dream.
Should the balsam fail,
all Araby
then holds nothing to help his cure.
Ask no further! I am weary!
(*She throws herself on the ground. A
train of squires and knights appears,
bearing and attending a litter.*)

GURNEMANZ

He comes. They bear him on the litter.
Oh woe! What sorrow pulls my heart-
strings
to see this king in bloom of manhood,
once ruler of a conq'ring race,
admitting sickness liege and lord!
(*to the squires*)
Be careful! Hear, the master groans.
(*The squires set down the litter.*)

AMFORTAS

(*raising himself a little*)
Right! So! My thanks! A little rest!
My night of pain has fled,
my morning joy has come!
The sacred lake's
cool waves will also help me,
will stint my woe.
The night of pain will lighten!
Gawain!

FIRST KNIGHT

Sir! Gawain left again;
for when his healing herb,
obtained through toilsome effort
did but betray your hopes,
he sallied forth again upon the venture.

AMFORTAS

Without leave? May he then repent it,
to keep so ill the Grail's command!
Oh woe to him, so rashly valiant,
if he should fall in Klingsor's toils!
Let no one break my peace with prob-
lems.
I wait for him, the promised Saviour,
"through pity, knowing,"
was't not thus?

GURNEMANZ

You said that it was thus.

AMFORTAS

"The holy fool" —
I think Death is that saviour,
did I but dare to name him!

GURNEMANZ

(*handing Amfortas the flask*)
Take of this: and see if it will help you.

AMFORTAS

Whence came this curious-looking
flask?

GURNEMANZ

Brought for your cure from Araby's
distant land.

AMFORTAS

And who obtained it?

GURNEMANZ

Right there the wild one lies.
Up, Kundry! Come!
(*Kundry refuses, and remains on the
ground.*)

AMFORTAS

You, Kundry?
Am I again to thank you,
you timid, restless soul?
Well then!
I'll take the balsam brought for me,
to show my thanks for such devotion.

KUNDRY

(*stirring uneasily on the ground*)
No thanks! Ha, ha! How will that help
one?
No thanks! Go, go! Your bath!
(*Amfortas gives the sign, and the pro-
cession disappears toward the valley.
Kundry remains crouching on the
ground. Squires pass to and fro.*)

THIRD SQUIRE

Hey you there!
Why lie you there like a brutish beast?

KUNDRY

Are the beasts here then not holy?

THIRD SQUIRE

Yes! But that you are so
is something we still don't know.

VIERTER KNAPPE

Mit ihrem Zaubersaft, wähn' ich,
wird sie den Meister vollends verderben.

GURNEMANZ

Hm! Schuf sie euch Schaden je?
Wann Alles ratlos steht
wie kämpfenden Brüdern in fernste
   Länder
Kunde sei zo entsenden,
und kaum ihr nur wisst, wohin?
Wer, ehe ihr euch nur besinnt,
stürmt und fliegt da hin und zurück,
der Botschaft pflegend mit Treu' und
   Glück?
Ihr nährt sie nicht, sie naht euch nie,
nichts hat sie mit euch gemein;
doch wann's in Gefahr der Hilfe gilt,
der Eifer führt sie schier durch die
   Luft,
die nie euch dann zum Danke ruft.
Ich wähne, ist dies Schaden,
so tät' er euch gut geraten?

DRITTER KNAPPE

Doch hasst sie uns.
Sieh' nur, wie hämisch dort nach uns
sie blickt!

VIERTER KNAPPE

Eine Heidin ist's, ein Zauberweib.

GURNEMANZ

Ja, eine Verwünschte mag sie sein.
Hier lebt sie heut',
vielleicht erneut,
zu büssen Schuld aus früh'rem Leben,
die dorten ihr noch nicht vergeben.
Uebt sie nun Buss' in solchen Taten,
die uns Ritterschaft zum Heil geraten,
gut tut sie dann ganz sicherlich,
dienet uns, und hilft auch sich.

DRITTER KNAPPE

Dann ist's wohl auch jen' ihre Schuld,
die uns so manche Not gebracht?

GURNEMANZ

Ja, wann oft lange sie uns ferne blieb,
dann brach ein Unglück wohl herein.
Und lang' schon kenn' ich sie:
doch Titurel kennt
sie noch länger.
Der fand, als er die Burg dort baute
sie schlafend hier im Waldgestrüpp',
erstarrt, leblos, wie tot.
So fand ich selbst sie letzlich wieder,
als uns das Unheil kaum gescheh'n,

das jener Böse über den Bergen
so schmählich über uns gebracht.
   (zu Kundry)
He! Du! Hör' mich und sag':
wo schweiftest damals du umher,
als unser Herr den Speer verlor?
   (Kundry schweigt.)
Warum halfst du uns damals nicht?

KUNDRY

Ich helfe nie.

VIERTER KNAPPE

Sie sagt's da selbst.

DRITTER KNAPPE

Ist sie so treu und kühn in Wehr,
so sende sie nach dem verlor'nen Speer!

GURNEMANZ

Das ist ein And'res: jedem ist's verwehrt.
   (mit grosser Ergriffenheit)
Oh, wunden-wundervoller heiliger
   Speer!
Ich sah dich schwingen von unheiligster Hand!
   (in Erinnerung sich verlierend)
Mit ihm bewehrt, Amfortas, Allzukühner,
wer mochte dir es wehren
den Zaub'rer zu beheeren!
Schon nah' dem Schloss, wird uns der
   Held entrückt:
ein furchtbar schönes Weib hat ihn
   entzückt:
in seinen Armen liegt er trunken,
der Speer ist ihm entsunken.
Ein Todesschrei! Ich stürm' herbei;
von dannen Klingsor lachend schwand,
den heil'gen Speer hatt' er entwandt.
Des Königs Flucht gab kämpfend ich
   Geleite;
doch eine Wunde brannt' ihm in der
   Seite:
die Wunde ist's, die nie sich schliessen
will.

DRITTER KNAPPE

So kanntest du Klingsor?

GURNEMANZ

(zu dem ersten und zweiten Knappen,
welche vom See her kommen)
Wie geht's dem König?

ERSTER KNAPPE

Ihn frischt das Bad.

FOURTH SQUIRE

And with her magic brew, perhaps,
she could cut off the life of our master.

GURNEMANZ

Hm! Has she done harm to you?
When we are all perplexed
how best to send tidings to far-off
 countries,
where our brothers are fighting,
we hardly know where, what then?
Who comes to your aid while you
 think,
flies away, and straightway is back,
a message bearer both tried and true?
She asks no food, and keeps away —
nothing's in common with you.
Yet when you need help, with danger
 near,
afire with duty she flies through the air.
She never even asks your thanks.
If this is what is harmful,
the harmful is what is helpful!

THIRD SQUIRE

She hates us though.
Just see the baleful glance she casts
 at us!

FOURTH SQUIRE

She's a heathen, sure; a sorceress!

GURNEMANZ

Yes, possibly burdened with a curse.
Here let her live.
She seems renewed,
repenting sin long since committed,
which at that time was not forgiven.
See, she atones in deeds of goodness
that both help and heal our noble
 knighthood.
Good are her deeds, and right,
 certainly:
good for us, and good for her.

THIRD SQUIRE

But is it not she we should blame,
she who has caused our want and woe?

GURNEMANZ

Yes, many times she ventures far away,
and when she goes our woe begins.
I knew her long ago,
but Titurel knew her still longer,
who found—that time he built the
 castle—
her sleeping in the underbrush,
benumbed, lifeless—as dead.
And thus again I found her lately,
just when that trouble came on us

which yonder wizard over the mountain
so shamefully did bring to pass.
 (to Kundry)
Hey, you! Hear me, and speak:
Where were you wandering about,
that time our lord had lost the spear?
(Kundry maintains a gloomy silence.)
Why did you not help us then?

KUNDRY

I never help.

FOURTH SQUIRE

She says't herself.

THIRD SQUIRE

If she's so true, so brave and bold,
then send her in quest of the missing
 spear!

GURNEMANZ

That's something diff'rent. That is not
 allowed.
 (with deep emotion)
Oh, wounding, wonderful and sanctified spear!
I saw you brandished by unsanctified
 hand!
 (becoming lost in remembrance)
Protected with it, Amfortas, all too
 valiant,
what power then could keep you
from laying low the wizard?
Our valiant king, while near the wall,
 is seized.
A gorgeous, fearsome witch holds him
 in thrall,
and her embraces make him drunken.
He lets the spear fall idly.
A frightful cry! I hurry there:
to see a laughing Klingsor leave.
The holy spear is gone with him.
I fought to help our king escape to
 safety;
but on his body now a wound was
 burning:
a wound so bad that it will never close!
(The first and second squires return
 from the lake.)

THIRD SQUIRE

So then you knew Klingsor?

GURNEMANZ

 (to the returning squires)
How fares our master?

FIRST SQUIRE

The bath was good.

ZWEITER KNAPPE

Dem Balsam wich das Weh?

GURNEMANZ

Die Wunde ist's, die nie sich schliessen
will!

DRITTER KNAPPE

Doch Väterchen sag' und lehr' uns
fein:
du kanntest Klingsor, wie mag das
sein?

(*Der dritte und der vierte Knappe hat-
ten sich zuletzt schon zu Gurnemanz'
Füssen niedergesetzt; die beiden anderen gesellen sich jetzt gleicher
Weise zu ihnen.*)

GURNEMANZ

Titurel, der fromme Held,
der kannt' ihn wohl.
Denn ihm, da wilder Feinde List und
Macht
des reinen Glauben's Reich bedrohten,
ihm neigten sich in heilig ernster Nacht
dereinst des Heiland's selige Boten:
daraus er trank beim letzten Liebesmahle,
das Weihgefäss, die heilig edle Schale,
darein am Kreuz sein göttlich Blut
auch floss,
dazu den Lanzenspeer, der dies vergoss,
der Zeugengüter höchstes Wundergut,
das gaben sie in unsres Königs Hut.
Dem Heiltum baute er das Heiligtum.
Die seinem Dienst ihr zugesindet
auf Pfaden, die kein Sünder findet,
ihr wisst, dass nur dem Reinen
vergönnt ist sich zu einen
den Brüdern, die zu höchsten Rettungs-
werken
des Grales heil'ge Wunderkräfte stär-
ken.
Drum blieb es dem, nach dem ihr
fragt, verwehrt,
Klingsor'n, wie hart ihn Müh' auch
drob beschwert.
Jenseits im Tale war er eingesiedelt;
darüber hin liegt üpp'ges Heidenland:
unkund blieb mir, was dorten er gesün-
digt;
doch wollt' er büssen nun, ja heilig
werden.
Ohnmächtig, in sich selbst die Sünde
zu ertöten,
an sich legt er die Frevlerhand,
die nun, dem Grale zugewandt,
verachtungsvoll dess' Hüter von sich
stiess,

Darob die Wut nun Klingsor'n unter-
wies,
wie seines schmählichen Opfers Tat
ihm gäbe zu bösem Zauber Rat;
den fand er nun.
Die Wüste schuf er sich zum Wonne-
garten
d'rinn wachsen teuflisch holde Frauen;
dort will des Grales Ritter er erwarten
zu böser Lust und Höllengrauen:
wen er verlockt, hat er erworben;
schon Viele hat er uns verdorben.
Da Titurel, in hohen Alter's Mühen,
dem Sohn die Herrschaft hier verlie-
hen,
Amfortas liess es da nicht ruh'n
der Zauberplag' Einhalt zu tun.
Das wisst ihr, wie es dort sich fand:
der Speer ist nun in Klingsor's Hand;
kann er selbst Heilige mit dem verwunden,
den Gral auch wähnt er fest schon uns
entwunden.

(*Kundry hat sich, in wütender Unruhe,
oft heftig umgewendet.*)

VIERTER KNAPPE

Vor Allem nun: der Speer kehr' uns
zurück!

DRITTER KNAPPE

Ha! Wer ihn brächt', ihm wär's zu
Ruhm und Glück!

GURNEMANZ

Vor dem verwaisten Heiligtum
in brünst'gem Beten lag Amfortas,
ein Rettungszeichen bang erflehend:
ein sel'ger Schimmer da entfloss dem
Grale;
ein heilig' Traumgesicht
nun deutlich zu ihm spricht
durch hell erschauter Wortezeichen
Male:
"Durch Mitleid wissend,
der reine Tor,
harre sein',
den ich erkor."

(*Vom See her hört man Geschrei und
Rufen.*)

RITTER UND KNAPPEN

Weh'! Weh! Hoho!
Auf! Wer ist der Frevler?

(*Gurnemanz und die vier Knappen
fahren auf und wenden sich er-
schrocken um.—Ein wilder Schwan
flattert matten Fluges vom See
daher; er ist verwundet, erhält sich*)

SECOND SQUIRE

The balsam eased his woe.

GURNEMANZ

A wound so bad that it will never close!

THIRD SQUIRE

Now fatherkin, speak and let us hear:
you knew the wizard, how could that be?

(*The third and fourth squires seat themselves at Gurnemanz's feet; the other two join them under the great tree.*)

GURNEMANZ

Titurel, the pious king,
knew Klingsor well.
There came a mighty heathen horde to threat
our realm of Christian faith — our stronghold;
but help arrived one sacred, solemn night.
Down came our Saviour's heavenly heralds:
the cup once used at that last holy supper,
that noble cup, that consecrated vessel,
wherein was caught His blood from off the cross;
thereto the holy lance which shed that blood.
These precious proofs of Love's great healing power
were given by angels to our ruler's care.
He gave these holy things a holy place.
And you, who serve by holy orders,
who took the path no sinner knows of,
you know the pure alone
are allowed to join the Brothers
in service, those devoted to the works
of salvation through the Grail's great power.
So, for the mage of whom you ask, he failed
outright, although he strove to enter in.
And then he settled in a lonely valley,
and all around was rankest heathen land.
What his sin was did never reach my knowledge.
His aim was penance though, yes, holy actions.
Yet lacking strength to slay the sins that were within him,
he laid rough hands upon himself
in hope that thus he'd gain the Grail.
But full of scorn our master spurned him forth.

For that was Klingsor seized with furious rage,
which made him turn his loathesome deed
to practice of wicked magic art,
which now he does.
The desert Klingsor made a pleasure garden
where flourish dev'lish lovely women.
There does he lie in waiting for the Grail knights,
with wicked lust and hellish torments.
Those whom he snares follow his banner.
Already he has ruined many.
Then Titurel, his body worn and waning,
empowered his son to take the kingdom.
Amfortas took no time to rest,
but tried to choke this wizard woe.
You know then what the sequel was:
the spear is now in Klingsor's hand,
which he can use to wound our holy knighthood.
Then he thinks to seize the holy chalice.

FOURTH SQUIRE

So first of all we must get back the spear.

THIRD SQUIRE

Whoso could, would win both fame and joy.

GURNEMANZ

Before the orphaned holy place
Amfortas knelt in ardent prayer,
imploring God a sign in answer.
A blessed shimm'ring flowed from out the chalice;
a holy, dreamlike face now clearly spoke to him
through bright-appearing, wondrous demonstration:
"Through pity, knowing—the holy fool.
Wait for him,
whom I ordained."

(*From the lake come cries and exclamations of the knights and squires. Gurnemanz and the four squires start up in alarm.*)

KNIGHTS AND SQUIRES (*off-stage*)

Woe! Woe! Ho-ho!
Up! Who is the miscreant?

(*A wild swan flutters feebly from over the lake. The squires and knights enter following it.*)

mühsam und sinkt endlich sterbend zu Boden.)

GURNEMANZ

Was gibt's?

ERSTER KNAPPE

Dort!

ZWEITER KNAPPE

Hier! Ein Schwan.

DRITTER KNAPPE

Ein wilder Schwan!

VIERTER KNAPPE

Er ist verwundet.

ANDERE KNAPPEN

(vom See her stürmend)

Ha! Wehe! Wehe!

GURNEMANZ

Wer schoss den Schwan?

ERSTER RITTER

Der König grüsst' ihn als gutes Zeichen.
als über'm See kreiste der Schwan:
da flog ein Pfeil.

NEUE KNAPPEN

(Parsifal vorführend)

Der war's! Der schoss! Dies der Bogen!
Hier der Pfeil, den seinen gleich.

GURNEMANZ

Bist du's, der diesen Schwan erlegte?

PARSIFAL

Gewiss! Im Fluge treff' ich, was fliegt!

GURNEMANZ

Du tatest das? Und bangt' es dich
nicht vor der Tat?

DIE KNAPPEN

Strafe den Frevler!

GURNEMANZ

Unerhörtes Werk!
Du konntest morden, hier im heil'gen
Walde,
dess' stiller Frieden dich umfing?
Des Haines Tiere nahten dir nicht
zahm.
Grüssten dich freundlich und fromm?
Aus den Zweigen was sangen die Vög-
lein dir?
Was tat dir der treue Schwan?
Sein Weibchen zu suchen flog der auf,
mit ihm zu kreisen über dem See;
den so er herrlich weihte zum Bad.

Dem stauntest du nicht? Dich lockt' es
nur
zu wild kindischem Bogengeschoss?
Er war uns hold: was ist er nun dir?
Hier schau' her! hier traf'st du ihn,
da starrt noch das Blut, matt hängen
die Flügel,
das Schneegefieder dunkel befleckt,
gebrochen das Aug', siehst du den
Blick?
Wirst deiner Sündentat du inne?

*(Parsifal hat ihm mit wachsender Er-
griffenheit zugehört: jetzt zerbricht
er seinen Bogen und schleudert die
Pfeile von sich.)*

Sag' Knab'! Erkennst du deine grosse
Schuld?

*(Parsifal führt die Hand über die
Augen.)*

Wie konntest du sie begeh'n?

PARSIFAL

Ich wusste sie nicht.

GURNEMANZ

Wo bist du her?

PARSIFAL

Das weiss ich nicht

GURNEMANZ

Wer ist dein Vater?

PARSIFAL

Das weiss ich nicht.

GURNEMANZ

Wer sandte dich dieses Weg's?

PARSIFAL

Das weiss ich nicht.

GURNEMANZ

Dein Name denn?

PARSIFAL

Ich hatte viele, doch weiss ich ihrer
keinen mehr.

GURNEMANZ

Das weisst du Alles nicht?
(für sich)
So dumm wie den erfand bisher ich
Kundry nur!
*(zu den Knappen, deren sich immer
mehre versammelt haben)*
Jetzt geht! Versäumt den König im
Bade nicht! Helft!

GURNEMANZ

What's up?

FOURTH SQUIRE

There!

THIRD SQUIRE

Here!

SECOND SQUIRE

A swan!

FOURTH SQUIRE

A forest swan!

THIRD SQUIRE

See! He is wounded!

ALL

Ha! Shameful! Shameful!

GURNEMANZ

Who shot the swan?
(*The swan, after painful flight, sinks
helplessly to earth. The second
knight draws an arrow from its
breast.*)

FIRST KNIGHT

Our master hailed it as a happy omen,
to see the swan circle the lake.
A shaft then flew! . . .
(*Knights and squires bring Parsifal in.*)

SQUIRES AND KNIGHTS

'Twas he! . . . who shot! See the bow
here!
Here's the shaft—just like the rest!

GURNEMANZ

It's you who dealt the swan its death-
blow?

PARSIFAL

Yes, I! In flight I hit all that flies.

GURNEMANZ

You slew the swan! And feel no horror
for your deed?

ALL

Punish the culprit!

GURNEMANZ

Execrable deed!
You could do murder? Here in sacred
forest,
whose silent peace enwrapped you
round,
whose woodland beasts approached you
without fear,
greeted you friendly and tame?
From the branches what warbled the
birds to you?
What harm did the faithful swan?
In seeking his mate he flew aloft
to circle with her over the lake,
thus nobly consecrating the bath.

This gave you no awe? Is all you want
a wild, puerile shot from your bow?
He had our love. What is he to you?
Here, just look! See where you hit!
There hardens his blood! Look!
    Wings hanging lifeless!
His snowy plumage flecked with the
stains!
No light in his eye! Notice the look?
(*Parsifal has listened to Gurnemanz
with increasing emotion. He now
breaks his bow to pieces and flings
the arrows from him.*)
Are you now conscious of your mis-
deed?
(*Parsifal draws his hand across his
eyes.*)
Speak, boy—are you aware of grievous
guilt?
Just how could you do this deed?

PARSIFAL

I did not know this.

GURNEMANZ

Where are you from?

PARSIFAL

I do not know.

GURNEMANZ

Who is your father?

PARSIFAL

I do not know.

GURNEMANZ

Who sent you to these environs?

PARSIFAL

I do not know.

GURNEMANZ

Then what's your name?

PARSIFAL

I once had many, but now I know not
what they are.

GURNEMANZ

You do not know at all?
        (*aside*)
I never knew one dumb as you — save
Kundry there!
(*to the squires, who have assembled in
still greater numbers*)
Now go! Do not neglect our king at
bath! Off!

(Die Knappen haben den Schwan ehrerbietig aufgenommen, und entfernen sich mit ihm jetzt nach dem See zu.)

GURNEMANZ

(sich wieder zu Parsifal wendend)

Nun sag': nichts weisst du, was ich
dich frage;
jetzt meld' was du weisst;
denn etwas musst du doch wissen.

PARSIFAL

Ich hab' eine Mutter; Herzeleide sie
heisst.
Im Wald und auf wilder Aue waren
wir heim.

GURNEMANZ

Wer gab dir den Bogen?

PARSIFAL

Den schuf ich mir selbst,
vom Forst die rauhen Adler zu verscheuchen.

GURNEMANZ

Doch adelig scheinst du selbst und
hochgeboren:
warum nicht liess deine Mutter
bessere Waffen dich lehren?

(Parsifal schweigt.)

KUNDRY

Den Vaterlosen gebar die Mutter,
als im Kampf erschlagen Gamuret!
Vor gleichem frühen Heldentod
den Sohn zu wahren, waffenfremd
in Oeden erzog sie ihn zum Toren—
die Törin!

(Sie lacht.)

PARSIFAL

(der mit jäher Aufmerksamkeit zugehört)

Ja! Und einst am Waldessaume vorbei,
auf schönen Tieren sitzend,
kamen glänzende Männer:
ihnen wollt' ich gleichen;
sie lachten und jagten davon.
Nun lief ich nach, doch konnt ich sie
nicht erreichen;
durch Wildnisse kam ich bergauf,
talab;
oft ward es Nacht, dann wieder Tag:
mein Bogen musste mir frommen
gegen Wild und grosse Männer . . .

KUNDRY

Ja! Schächer und Riesen traf seine
Kraft;
den freislichen Knaben lernten sie
fürchten.

PARSIFAL

Wer fürchtet mich? Sag'!

KUNDRY

Die Bösen!

PARSIFAL

Die mich bedrohten, waren sie bös'?

(Gurnemanz lacht.)

Wer ist gut?

GURNEMANZ

(ernst)

Deine Mutter, der du entlaufen,
und die um dich sich nun härmt und
grämt.

KUNDRY

Zu End' ihr Gram: seine Mutter ist
tot.

PARSIFAL

(in furchtbarem Schrecken)

Tot? Meine Mutter? Wer sagt's?

KUNDRY

Ich ritt vorbei, und sah sie sterben:
dich Toren hiess sie mich grüssen.

*(Parsifal springt wütend auf Kundry
zu und fasst sie bei der Kehle.)*

GURNEMANZ

(ihn zurückhaltend)

Verrückter Knabe! Wieder Gewalt?
Was tat dir das Weib? Es sagte wahr,
denn nie lügt Kundry, doch sah sie
viel.

*(Nach dem Gurnemanz Kundry befreit,
steht Parsifal lange wie erstarrt; dann
gerät er in ein heftiges Zittern.)*

PARSIFAL

Ich verschmachte!

*(Kundry ist hastig an einen Waldquell
gesprungen, bringt jetzt Wasser in
einem Horne, besprengt damit zunächst Parsifal, und reicht ihm dann
zu trinken.)*

GURNEMANZ

So recht! So nach des Grales Gnade:
das Böse bannt, wer's mit Gutem vergilt.

(*The squires place the dead swan reverently on a bier of green boughs and bear it away toward the lake. Finally only Gurnemanz, Parsifal, and—apart—Kundry, remain. Gurnemanz turns to Parsifal.*)

Now speak! Since you know nothing I asked you,
just tell what you know—for surely you must know something.

KUNDRY

Yes! Robbers and giants sampled its strength.
The valorous stripling taught them to fear him.

PARSIFAL

Who had this fear? Who?

KUNDRY

The wicked!

PARSIFAL

Then those who threatened—were they then bad?
(*Gurnemanz laughs.*)
Who is good?

PARSIFAL

Yes! I have a mother, Heart of Sorrow her name.
I know that a wild and trackless moor was our home.

GURNEMANZ

Who gave you your weapon?

PARSIFAL

I made it myself, to scare the savage eagles from the forest.

GURNEMANZ

Yet you seem eagle too, and born most nobly.
Why did your mother not let you handle
a weapon more manly?
(*Parsifal is silent.*)

GURNEMANZ (*seriously*)

Your dear mother, whom you deserted, and who now pines and grieves for you.

KUNDRY

Her grief is done, for his mother is dead.

PARSIFAL (*in fearful horror*)

Dead? My mother? Says who?

KUNDRY

Once riding by I saw her dying.
And, fool, she sent you her greeting.
(*Parsifal springs enraged at Kundry and seizes her by the throat. Gurnemanz holds him back.*)

GURNEMANZ

You rascally youngster! Always with force!
(*After Gurnemanz has released Kundry, Parsifal stands awhile as if petrified.*)
Now, what has she done? She spoke the truth.
For though she sees much, she never lies.

KUNDRY

His father Gamuret died in battle,
so he only knows a mother's care.
To save him from like hero's death,
she raised him cloistered in the wild,
a fool now, and ignorant of weapons.
(*She laughs.*)
More fool she!

PARSIFAL

(*who has listened with keen attention*)

Yes! One day I saw some glittering men
that rode along the forest's edge
on beautiful horses.
I desired to be like them.
They laughed, and they galloped away.
I ran quite fast, but never could overtake them.
I traveled on, through woods, up hill, down dale.
Oft came the night, then day again.
My weapon had to protect me
from strong men and savage creatures . . .

PARSIFAL

(*falling into violent trembling*)

I am fainting!
(*Kundry, on perceiving Parsifal's condition, hastens to a brook, brings water in a horn, and sprinkles Parsifal with it, giving him some to drink.*)

GURNEMANZ

That's right! So, as the Grail inspires us!
The evil ends, when repaid with the good.

KUNDRY

(*traurig sich abwendend*)

Nie tu' ich Gutes; nur Ruhe will ich.

(*Während Gurnemanz sich väterlich um Parsifal bemüht, schleppt sich Kundry, von Beiden unbeachtet, einem Waldgebüsche zu.*)

Nur Ruhe, ach, der Müden.
Schlafen! Oh, dass mich keiner wecke!

(*scheu auffahrend*)

Nein! Nicht schlafen! Grausen fasst mich!
Machtlose Wehr! Die Zeit ist da.
Schlafen—schlafen—ich muss.

(*Sie sinkt hinter dem Gebüsch zusammen.*)

GURNEMANZ

Vom Bade kehrt der König heim;
hoch steht die Sonne:
nun lass' zum frommen Mahle mich
dich geleiten;
denn, bist du rein,
wird nun der Gral dich tränken und speisen.

(*Er hat Parsifal's Arm sich sanft um den Nacken gelegt, und hält dessen Leib mit seinem eigenen Arme umschlungen; so geleitet er ihn bei sehr allmählichem Schreiten.*)

PARSIFAL

Wer ist der Gral?

GURNEMANZ

Das sagt sich nicht:
doch bist du selbst zu ihm erkoren,
bleibt dir die Kunde unverloren.
Und sieh'!
Mich dünkt, dass ich dich recht erkannt:
kein Weg führt zu ihm durch das Land,
und Niemand könnte ihn beschreiten,
den er nicht selber möcht' geleiten.

PARSIFAL

Ich schreite kaum,
doch wähn' ich mich schon weit.

GURNEMANZ

Du siehst, mein Sohn,
zum Raum wird hier die Zeit.

(*Allmählich, während Gurnemanz und Parsifal zu schreiten scheinen, verwandelt sich die Bühne, in unmerklicher Weise: es verschwindet so der Wald; in Felsenwänden öffnet sich*

ein Tor, welches nun die Beiden einschliesst. Endlich sind sie in einem mächtigen Saale angekommen welcher nach oben in eine hochgewölbte Kuppel, durch die einzig das Licht hereindringt, sich verliert.)

Jetzt achte wohl; und lass' mich seh'n.
bist du ein Tor und rein,
welch Wissen dir auch mag beschieden sein.

(*Auf beiden Seiten des Hintergrundes wird je eine grosse Tür geöffnet. Von rechts schreiten die Ritter des Grales, in feierlichem Zuge, herein, und reihen sich, nach und nach an zwei überdeckten langen Speisetafeln, welche so gestellt sind, dass sie die Mitte des Saales frei lassen: nur Becher, keine Gerichte stehen darauf.*)

DIE GRALSRITTER

Zum letzten Liebesmahle
gerüstet Tag für Tag,
gleich ob zum letzten Male
es heut' uns letzen mag,
wer guter Tat sich freu't,
ihm wird das Mahl erneu't.
der Labung darf er nah'n,
die hehrste Gab' empfah'n.

JÜNGERE MÄNNERSTIMMEN

Den sündigen Welten
mit tausend Schmerzen
wie einst sein Blut geflossen,
dem Erlösungshelden
mit freudigem Herzen
sie nun mein Blut vergossen.
Der Leib, den er zur Sühn' uns bot,
er leb' in uns durch seinen Tod.

KNABENSTIMMEN

Der Glaube lebt;
Die Taube schwebt,
des Heiland's holder Bote:
der für euch fliesst,
des Weines geniesst,
und nehmt vom Lebensbrote!

Als alle Ritter an den Tafeln ihre Sitze eingenommen haben, tritt ein längeres Stillschweigen ein.—Vom Hintergrunde her vernimmt man, aus einer gewölbten Nische hinter dem Ruhebette des Amfortas, wie aus einem Grabe die Stimme des alten

TITUREL

Mein Sohn Amfortas bist du am Amt?

KUNDRY *(gloomily)*

Good do I never.

*(She turns sadly away and while Gur-
nemanz is attending to Parsifal with
fatherly care, she crawls, unper-
ceived, toward a thicket.)*

It's rest I long for.
Just rest, ah! Ah! This tiredness!
Sleep now! Oh, would that none might
wake me!
No! No sleep now! Terror grips me!

*(She trembles violently; her arms drop
powerlessly.)*

Vain to resist! The time has come!
Sleep now! Sleep now! I must!

(She sinks down behind the thicket.)

GURNEMANZ

The king has had his bath and comes.
The sun's at highest.
Now let me lead the way to our pious
supper,
for if you're pure,
the Holy Grail will quench you and
feed you.

*(Gurnemanz gently lays Parsifal's arm
on his own neck, and supporting
him, leads him slowly along. The
scene begins to change.)*

PARSIFAL

Who is the Grail?

GURNEMANZ

I may not tell.
But if you're chosen for its service,
you'll know the truth that brings you
knowledge.
And see!
I think that I do know you now.
No way leads to it through the land,
and no one could so guide his footsteps,
unless the Grail itself did show him.

PARSIFAL

I hardly walk,
yet seem t'have gone quite far.

GURNEMANZ

You see, my son,
that here time turns to space.

*(As Parsifal and Gurnemanz appear to
walk, the scene changes more and
more visibly. The forest disappears
and a doorway appears in rocky
walls concealing the two. The two*

*enter the vast hall of the Grail castle.
We see a pillared hall with a high
dome in the center over the refec-
tory. Enter the knights of the Grail,
who take their places at the tables.)*

Now heed me well and let me see,
— if you're a fool, and pure —
what knowledge will be granted you
by grace.

THE GRAIL KNIGHTS

This sacred meal is daily.
Each time is as the last.
Our God sustains us truly
In this divine repast.

*(A second train of squires crosses the
hall.)*

Who joys in deeds of love
New food gains from Above.
Who dares approach the Grail,
Will through its light prevail.

*(The assembled knights place them-
selves at the tables. Voices of young-
er men, coming from the mid-height
of the hall, are heard. Through the
opposite door Amfortas is brought in
on a litter by squires and serving
brethren. Before him march the four
squires bearing the draped shrine.
The procession wends to the center
of the background, where a raised
couch stands. On this Amfortas is
placed. Before it is a longish stone
table on which the boys set down
the Grail.)*

BOYS' VOICES

As once our dear Master
In love for mankind
His blood in anguish offered,
So in happy rapture,
With love in turn for my Saviour
My blood's now proffered.
The Christ, whose blood for us did
pay,
Now lives in us and heals today.

BOYS' VOICES

Our God is Love,
And sends the dove,
Harmonious peace revealing;
Take of the wine,
Perception divine,
And bread that brings you healing.

*(When all have taken their seats and
there is a pause, from the distance,
behind Amfortas' couch, is heard
Titurel's voice.)*

TITUREL'S VOICE

My son Amfortas, do you still serve?

Soll ich den Gral heut' noch erschau'n
und leben?

(*Schweigen*)

Muss ich sterben, vom Retter unge-
leitet?

AMFORTAS

(*im Ausbruche qualvoller Verzweiflung*)

Wehe! Wehe mir der Qual!
Mein Vater, oh! noch einmal
verrichte du das Amt!
Lebe, leb' und lass' mich sterben!

TITUREL

Im Grabe leb' ich durch des Heiland's
Huld:
zu schwach doch bin ich ihm zu dienen.
Du büss' im Dienste deine Schuld!
Enthüllet den Gral!

AMFORTAS

(*den Knaben wehrend*)

Nein! Lasst ihn unenthüllt! Oh!
Dass Keiner, Keiner diese Qual ermisst,
die mir der Anblick weckt, der euch
entzückt!
Was ist die Wunde, ihrer Schmerzen
Wut,
gegen die Not, die Höllenpein,
zu diesem Amt verdammt zu sein!
Wehvolles Erbe, dem ich verfallen,
ich, einziger Sünder unter Allen,
des höchsten Heiligtum's zu pflegen,
auf Reine herabzuflehen seinen Segen!
Oh, Strafe! Strafe ohne Gleichen
des, ach! gekränkten Gnadenreichen!
Nach Ihm, nach Seinem Weihegrusse
muss sehnlich mich's verlangen;
aus tiefster Seele Heilesbusse
zu Ihm muss ich gelangen.
Die Stunde naht:
ein Lichstrahl senkt sich auf das heilig'
Werk:
die Hülle fällt.
Des Weihgefässes göttlicher Gehalt
erglüht mit leuchtender Gewalt;
durchzückt von seligsten Genusses
Schmerz,
des heiligsten Blutes Quell
fühl' ich sich giessen in mein Herz:
des eig'nen sündigen Blutes Gewell'
in wahnsinniger Flucht
muss mir zurück dann fliessen,
in die Welt der Sündenzucht
mit wilder Scheu sich ergiessen:
von Neuem sprengt er das Tor,
daraus es nun strömt hervor,

hier durch die Wunde, der Seinen
gleich,
geschlagen von desselben Speeres
Streich,
der dort dem Erlöser die Wunde stach,
aus der mit blutigen Tränen
der Göttliche weint' ob der Menschheit
Schmach
in Mitleid's heiligem Sehnen,
und aus der nun mir, an heiligster
Stelle,
dem Pfleger göttlichster Güter,
des Erlösungsbalsam's Hüter,
das heisse Sündenblut entquillt,
ewig erneu't aus des Sehnen's Quelle,
das, ach! keine Büssung je mir stillt!
Erbarmen! Erbarmen!
Du Allerbarmer, ach! Erbarmen!
Nimm mir mein Erbe,
schliesse die Wunde,
dass heilig ich sterbe,
rein Dir gesunde!

(*Er sinkt wie bewusstlos zurück.*)

KNABENSTIMMEN

(*aus der Kuppel*)

"Durch Mitleid wissend,
der reine Tor:
harre sein',
den ich erkor."

DIE RITTER

So ward es dir verhiessen, harre getrost;
des Amtes walte heut'!

TITUREL'S STIMME

Enthüllet den Gral!

(*Amfortas hat sich schweigend wieder
erhoben. Die Knaben entkleiden den
goldenen Schrein, entnehmen ihm
den "Gral" (eine antike Krystal-
schale), von welchem sie ebenfalls
eine Verhüllung abnehmen, und setz-
en ihn vor Amfortas hin.*)

TITUREL'S STIMME

Der Segen!

(*Während Amfortas andachtsvoll in
stummem Gebete sich zu dem Kelche
neigt, verbreitet sich eine immer
dichtere Dämmerung im Saale.*)

KNABEN (*aus der Kuppel*)

"Nehmet hin meinen Leib
nehmet hin mein Blut
um unsrer Liebe Willen!
Nehmet hin mein Blut,
Nehmet hin meinen Leib
auf dass ihr mein' gedenkt."

Shall I again look to the Grail to heal me?

(long pause)

Must I die then, unguided by my Saviour?

AMFORTAS
(half raising himself, in a despairing outburst)

Torment! Torment! Endless pain!
Oh Father, once more perform
what the Holy Grail requires.
Carry on, and let me perish!

TITUREL'S VOICE

I live entombed through our Redeemer's grace,
too feeble now to ever serve Him.
Make your atonement for your guilt.
Uncover the Grail!

AMFORTAS (restraining the boys)

No! Let it stay concealed.
Oh, that no one, no one here should know my pain,
caused by the sacred sight that gives you joy.
What is the spear wound and its torment
compared to the pain, the hellish hurt
of being condemned to serve the Grail?
Dolorous duty on me has fallen.
I—only sinner in the knighthood,
must tend this highest holy relic
and call down its blessing upon the pure ones!
Infliction! Punishment unequaled
from — ah! — the troubled Fount of Mercy!
For Him and for His benediction,
my eager heart is yearning.
My inmost soul desires atonement from God,
our only Saviour.
The hour draws near.
The light streams down upon the sanctified work.
The covering falls.
The vessel's holy contents glow again
with healing power upon us all.
I feel a rapturous and rending pain
that comes from our Saviour's blood,
which pours itself into my heart.
The furious tide of my own sinning blood
deliriously rushes back in surging torrents,
for it seeks this world of lust
to pour itself out headlong.
Again it forces the door,
again it emerges forth,

here through this lance wound—like unto His,
inflicted by the stab of that same spear,
which gave our Redeemer the holy wound,
and bloodstained tears of anguish
the Son of Man shed for all mankind's shame,
with tender, pitiful yearning.
And now too from me, in holiest office,
the guard of godliest relics
and of healing balm from heaven,
my fev'rish, sinful blood flows forth,
ever renewed from that sensual fountain
which — ah! — no repentance ever stills.
Have mercy! Have mercy!
God of Mercy, show me mercy!
Free me from service,
save me and heal me,
that I may die holy,
pure — with salvation!

(He sinks back as if unconscious.)

BOYS, YOUNG MEN FROM THE HEIGHT
"Made wise through pity,
the holy fool.
Wait for him,
the one I chose."

THE KNIGHTS

Such were the words predicted.
Wait and believe. Perform your office still.

TITUREL'S VOICE

Uncover the Grail!

(Amfortas raises himself slowly and painfully. The boys remove the covering from the golden shrine, take out an antique crystal cup, from which they also remove a covering, and set it before Amfortas.)

The blessing!

BOY'S VOICES (from above)

"Take my body and eat.
Take my blood and drink.
This is my loving order."

(While Amfortas bows himself before the Cup in prayer, an increasing gloom spreads in the hall, culminating in complete darkness.)

"Take my blood and drink,
Take my body and eat.
Do this in thought of me."

(Ein blendender Lichstrahl dringt von oben auf die Schale herab, diese erglüht immer stärker in leuchtender Purpurfarbe. Amfortas, mit verklärter Miene, erhebt den "Gral" hoch und schwenkt ihn sanft nach allen Seiten hin. Alles ist bereits bei dem Eintritte der Dämmerung auf die Knie gesunken, und erhebt jetzt die Blicke andächtig zum "Grale.")

TITUREL'S STIMME

Oh! Heilig Wonne!
Wie hell grüsst uns heute der Herr!

(Amfortas setzt den "Gral" wieder nieder, welcher nun, während die tiefe Dämmerung wieder entweicht, immer mehr erblasst: hierauf schliessen die Knaben das Gefäss wieder in den Schrein, und bedecken diesen, wie zuvor.—Mit dem Wiedereintritte der vorigen Tageshelle sind auf den Speisetafeln die Becher, jetzt mit Wein gefüllt, wieder deutlich geworden, neben jedem liegt ein Brot. Alles lässt sich zum Mahle nieder, so auch Gurnemanz, welcher einen Platz neben sich leer hält und Parsifal durch ein Zeichen zur Teilnehmung am Mahle einlädt: Parsifal bleibt aber starr und stumm wie gänzlich entrückt, zur Seite stehen.)

KNABENSTIMMEN

Wein und Brot des letzten Mahles
wandelt' einst der Herr des Grales,
durch des Mitleid's Liebesmacht,
in das Blut, das er vergoss,
in den Leib, den dar er bracht'.

JÜNGLINGSSTIMMEN

Blut und Leib der heil' gen Gabe
wandelt heut' zu eurer Labe
sel'ger Tröstung Liebesgeist,
in den Wein, der euch nun floss,
in das Brot, das heut' euch speis't.

DIE RITTER
(Erste Hälfte)

Nehmet vom Brot,
wandelt es kühn
zu Leibes Kraft und Stärke;
treu bis zum Tod,
fest jedem Müh'n,
zu wirken des Heiland's Werke.
(Zweite Hälfte)
Nehmet vom Wein,
Wandelt ihn neu

zu Lebens feurigem Blute,
froh im Verein,
brudertreu
zu kämpfen mit seligem Mute.

(Sie erheben sich feierlich und reichen einander die Hände.)

ALLE RITTER

Selig im Glauben!
Selig in Liebe!

JÜNGLINGE
(aus mittler Höhe)

Selig in Liebe!

KNABEN
(aus oberster Höhe)

Selig im Glauben!

(Während des Mahles, an welchem er nicht teilnahm ist Amfortas aus seiner begeisterungsvollen Erhebung allmählich wieder herabgesunken: er neigt das Haupt und hält die Hand auf die Wunde. Die Knaben nähern sich ihm; ihre Bewegungen deuten auf das erneuerte Bluten der Wunde: sie pflegen Amfortas, geleiten ihn wieder auf die Sänfte, und, während Alle sich zum Aufbruch rüsten, tragen sie, in der Ordnung wie sie kamen, Amfortas und den heiligen Schrein wieder von dannen. Die Ritter und Knappen reihen sich ebenfalls wieder zum feierlichen Zuge, und verlassen langsam den Saal, aus welchem die vorherige Tageshelle allmählich weicht. Die Glocken haben wieder geläutet. —

Parsifal hatte bei dem vorangegangenen stärksten Klagerufe des Amfortas eine heftige Bewegung nach dem Herzen gemacht, welches er krampfhaft eine Zeit lang gefasst hielt; jetzt steht er noch wie erstarrt, regungslos da.—Als die Letzten den Saal verlassen, und die Türen wieder geschlossen sind, tritt Gurnemanz missmutig an Parsifal heran, und rüttelt ihn am Arme.)

GURNEMANZ

Was stehst du noch da?
Weisst du, was du sah'st?

(Parsifal schüttelt ein wenig sein Haupt.)

Du bist doch eben nur ein Tor!

(Er öffnet eine schmale Seitentüre.)

(A blinding ray of light shoots down from above upon the Cup, which then glows with an increasing purple luster, shedding a soft radiance on all around. Amfortas, with brightened mien, raises the Grail aloft and waves it gently about, blessing the bread and wine. All kneel.)

TITUREL'S VOICE

Oh! Rapture from heaven,
how joyful today is the Word!

(Amfortas sets down the Grail again, which now, while the deep gloom wanes, grows paler. The boys cover it as before, and return it to the shrine, which they also veil. The former daylight returns. The four boys apportion, during the following, bread and wine from two baskets and two pitchers.)

BOYS

Wine and bread to substance changing,
This the Grail's dear Lord's arranging,
Through the power of Love divine,
Into bread that is His flesh,
Into blood of that true Vine.

YOUNG MEN

Blood and flesh, as His creation,
Show His love, our true Salvation.
God is Spirit, God is Love,
God inspires with Wine from Heaven,
God is manna from Above.

THE KNIGHTS

FIRST HALF

Take of the bread,
Quickening power,
For with it strength is given.
True to the death,
Now is the hour
To follow the will of heaven.

SECOND HALF

Take of the wine,
Change it anew,
To blood of zealous defiance.

ALL KNIGHTS

Right is divine,
Brotherhood true,
So battle with holy reliance!

YOUNG MEN

Love is our Saviour.

BOYS

Faith is our fortress.

(The knights rise and advance from opposite sides solemnly to embrace one another. During the meal, of which he has not partaken, Amfortas gradually relapses from his state of exaltation; he droops his head and presses his hand to the wound. The boys approach him, their actions denoting the wound has burst out afresh. They tend him and assist him to his litter. Then, while all prepare to leave, they bear off Amfortas and the shrine in the order in which they came. The knights and squires fall in, and slowly quit the hall in solemn procession. The procession with Amfortas disappears. Waning daylight returns. Squires again march quickly through the hall. They disappear and the doors are closed. Parsifal, on hearing Amfortas' last cry of agony, clutches his heart and remains in that position for some time.)

GURNEMANZ

(ill-humoredly shaking Parsifal by the arm)

You stand like a stock.
Just what have you seen?

(Parsifal, still clutching his heart, shakes his head slightly.)

You are then nothing but a fool!
Leave the place! Away with you!

(He opens a narrow side door.)

Dort hinaus deinem Wege zu!
Doch rät dir Gurnemanz,
lass' du hier künfig die Schwäne in
   Ruh',
und suche dir Gänser die Gans!

*Er stösst Parsifal hinaus und schlägt,
ärgerlich, hinter ihm die Türe stark
zu. Während er dann den Rittern
folgt, schliesst sich der Bühnenvor-
hang.*

ZWEITER AUFZUG

KLINGSOR'S ZAUBERSCHLOSS

*Im inneren Verliesse eines nach oben
offenen Turmes: Steinstufen führen
nach dem Zinnenrande der Turmmauer; Finsternis in der Tiefe,
nach welcher es von dem Mauervorsprunge hinabführt. Zauber-
werkzeuge und nekromantische
Vorrichtungen. Klingsor auf dem
Mauervorsprunge zur Seite, vor
einem Metallspiegel sitzend.*

KLINGSOR

Die Zeit ist da,
Schon lockt mein Zauberschloss den
   Toren,
den, kindisch jauchzend, fern ich nahen
   seh'.
Im Todesschlafe hält der Fluch sie
   fest,
der ich den Krampf zu lösen weiss.
Auf denn! An's Werk!

*(Er steigt, der Mitte zu, etwas tiefer
hinab, und entzündet dort Räucher-
werk, welches alsbald einen Teil des
Hintergrundes mit einem bläulichen
Dampfe erfüllt. Dann setzt er sich
wieder an die vorige Stelle, und ruft,
mit geheimnissvollen Gebärden, nach
dem Abgrunde.)*

Herauf! Hieher! zu mir!
Dein Meister ruft dich Namenlose:
Ur-Teufelin! Höllen-Rose!
Herodias war'st du, und was noch?
Gundryggia dort, Kundry hier!
Hieher! Hieher denn, Kundry!
Dein Meister ruft: herauf!

*(In dem bläulichen Lichte steigt Kun-
dry's Gestalt herauf. Man hört sie
einen grässlichen Schrei ausstossen,
wie eine aus tiefstem Schlafe auf-
geschreckte Halbwache.)*

Erwach'st du? Ha!
Meinem Banne wieder
verfallen heut' zur rechten Zeit.

*(Kundry lässt ein Klagegeheul, von
grösster Heftigkeit bis zu bangem
Wimmern sich abstufend, verneh-
men.)*

Sag', wo trieb'st du dich wieder umher?
Pfui! Dort, bei dem Ritter-Gesipp',
wo wie ein Vieh du dich halten lässt!
Gefällt dir's bei mir nicht besser?
Als ihren Meister du mir gefangen —
ha ha! den reinen Hüter des Grales
was jagte dich da wieder fort?

KUNDRY

*(rauh und abgebrochen, wie im Ver-
suche, wieder Sprache zu gewinnen)*

Ach! Ach!
Tiefe Nacht —
Wahnsinn! Oh! Wut!
Ach! Jammer!
Schlaf—Schlaf—
tiefer Schlaf! Tod!

KLINGSOR

Da weckte dich ein And'rer? He?

KUNDRY *(wie zuvor)*

Ja! Mein Fluch!
Oh! Sehnen—Sehnen!

KLINGSOR

Ha ha! dort nach den keuschen Rittern.

KUNDRY

Da—da—dient' ich.

KLINGSOR

Ja, ja! den Schaden zu vergüten,
den du ihnen böslich gebracht?
Sie helfen dir nicht;
feil sind sie Alle,
biet' ich den rechten Preis:
der festeste fällt,
sinkt er dir in die Arme
und so verfällt er dem Speer,
den ihrem Meister selbst ich entwandt.
Den Gefährlichsten gilt's nun heut' zu
   besteh'n:
ihn schirmt der Torheit Schild.

KUNDRY

Ich—will nicht! Oh! Oh!

KLINGSOR

Wohl willst du, denn du musst.

KUNDRY

Du kannst mich nicht halten.

Yet hark to Gurnemanz:
Hereafter do not go after our swans.
Just seek—foolish gander—a goose!

(*He pushes Parsifal out and slams the
door after him. As he himself turns
to follow the knights, the curtain
falls.*)

ACT II

*Klingsor's magic castle, inner dungeon
of a tower open at the top. Stone
stairs lead to the edge of the battle-
ments. Darkness in lower part of
scene. Instruments of magic and
necromancy. Klingsor is seated before a metal mirror.*

KLINGSOR

The time has come.
The boy now nears with childish out-
cries.
My magic castle lures the lad this way.
A deathly slumber still binds fast my
slave,
so let me end her cramping curse.
Up then! To work!

(*He steps down, kindles incense, which
immediately fills the background
with a bluish light, then seats himself before the magical apparatus
and with mystical gestures calls down
into the abyss.*)

Get up! Get up! Come here!
Your master calls you, nameless crea-
ture,
First sorceress! Rose of Hades!
Herodias one time, and what else?
Gundrygia there, Kundry here!
Come here! Come here then, Kundry!
Your master calls: arise!

(*Kundry's figure rises up through the
bluish light. She appears asleep, then
gives signs of awakening. She utters
a fearful cry.*)

You're wak'ning? Ha!
You have fallen again to my spell today
—in time of need.

(*Kundry utters a loud lament that
diminishes to a whimper.*)

Say, where have you been roaming
again?
Pfui! There, by that rabble of knights,
where you are looked upon as a beast!
With me don't you fare much better?
You lured their master into my power
— ha ha! — the virgin guard of the
chalice,
so what was it drove you away?

KUNDRY

(*hoarsely, and in broken sounds as if
seeking to regain speech*)

Ah! Ah!
Gloomy night—
Madness!—Oh!—Rage!—
Oh! Anguish—
Sleep—sleep—
Deepest sleep!—Death!

KLINGSOR

Then did another wake you? Hey?

KUNDRY (*as before*)

Yes!—My curse!
Oh!—Longing—longing!

KLINGSOR

Ha! ha! there—for the virgin knighthood?

KUNDRY

There—I—served them.

KLINGSOR

Yes, yes! You thought to make repay-
ment for harm you had done to the
band?
But they cannot help;
all are corrupted—
if I just ask their price.
The firmest will fall,
yielding to your embraces,
and then be quelled by the spear,
which from their lord himself I pur-
loined.
Our most dangerous foe is due on this
day:
one armed with folly's shield.

KUNDRY

I—will not. No! No!

KLINGSOR

You will well, for you must.

KUNDRY

You cannot compel me.

KLINGSOR

Aber dich fassen.

KUNDRY

Du?

KLINGSOR

Dein Meister.

KUNDRY

Aus welcher Macht?

KLINGSOR

Ha! Weil einzig an mir
deine Macht nichts vermag.

KUNDRY (*grell lachend*)

Ha! ha! —Bist du keusch?

KLINGSOR (*wütend*)

Was fräg'st du das, verfluchtes Weib?
Furchtbare Not!
So lacht nun der Teufel mein,
dass einst ich nach dem Heiligen rang?
Furchtbare Not!
Ungebändigten Sehnens Pein!
Schrecklichster Triebe Höllendrang,
den ich zum Todesschweigen mir
   zwang,
lacht und höhnt er nun laut
durch dich, des Teufels Braut?
Hüte dich!
Hohn und Verachtung büsste schon
   Einer,
der Stolze, stark in Heiligkeit,
der einst mich von sich stiess,
sein Stamm verfiel mir, unerlöst
soll der Heiligen Hüter mir schmachten;
und bald, so wähn' ich,
hüt' ich mir selbst den Gral.
Ha! Ha!
Gefiel er dir wohl, Amfortas, der Held,
den ich dir zur Wonne gesellt?

KUNDRY

Oh! Jammer! Jammer!
Schwach auch Er, schwach Alle,
Meinem Fluche mit mir
Alle verfallen!
Oh, ewiger Schlaf,
einziges Heil,
wie, wie dich gewinnen?

KLINGSOR

Ha! Wer dir trotzte, lös'te dich frei:
versuch's mit dem Knaben, der nah't!

KUNDRY

Ich will nicht!

KLINGSOR

(*ist auf die Turmmauer gestiegen*)

Jetzt schon erklimmt er die Burg.

KUNDRY

Oh Wehe! Wehe!
Erwachte ich darum?
Muss ich? Muss?

KLINGSOR

(*hinabblickend*)

Ha! Er ist schön, der Knabe!

KUNDRY

Oh!—Oh!—Wehe mir!

KLINGSOR

(*stösst in ein Horn*)

Ho! Ihr Wächter! Ho! Ritter!
Helden! Auf! Feinde nah'!
Hei! Wie zur Mauer sie stürmen,
die betörten Eigenholde,
zum Schutz ihres schönen Geteufel's!
So! Mutig! Mutig!
Haha! Der fürchtet sich nicht:
dem Helden Ferris entwand er die
   Waffe;
die führt er nun freislich wider den
   Schwarm.
(*Kundry beginnt unheimlich zu lach-
en.*)
Wie übel den Tölpeln der Eifer ge-
deih't!
Dem schlug er den Arm, jenem den
   Schenkel.
Haha! Sie weichen! Sie fliehen!
Seine Wunde trägt Jeder nach heim!
Wie das ich euch gönne!
Möge denn so
das ganze Rittergezücht
unter sich selber sich würgen!
Ha! Wie stolz er nun steht auf der
   Zinne!
Wie lachen ihm die Rosen der Wangen,
da kindisch erstaunt
in den einsamen Garten er blickt!
He! Kundry!

(*Er wendet sich um. Kundry ist plötzlich verschwunden; das bläuliche
Licht ist erloschen: volle Finsterniss
in der Tiefe.*)

Wie? Schon am Werk?
Haha! Den Zauber wusst' ich wohl,
der immer dich wieder zum Dienst mir
   gesellt.
Du da, kindischer Spross,
was auch
Weissagung dir wies,

KLINGSOR

But I can seize you.

KUNDRY

You!

KLINGSOR

Your master.

KUNDRY

And by what power?

KLINGSOR

Ha! The power of a man
who's immune to your charms.

KUNDRY

Ha! ha! Are you chaste?

KLINGSOR

And why ask that, accursed witch?
  Horrible lack!
So laughs the devil now
because I strove for holiness once!
  Horrible lack!
Irrepressible longing pain!
Terrible pricking lust from hell
—which once I quelled to quiet of
  death—
laughs and mocks me aloud
through you, the devil's bride! Have
  a care!
Well did he pay for scorn and derision
—that proud one—strong in holiness,
who spurned me from him once.
His stock is blasted.
Unredeemed
shall the holy custodian suffer;
and soon, I fancy,
I shall be lord of the Grail—
Haha!
And did you not like Amfortas, the
  brave,
he whom I gave you for your joy?

KUNDRY

Oh! Torment! Torment!
Weak—he too! All weaklings!
For the curse I bear
brings all to their ruin—
Oh, sleep without end,
only release,
how, how may I win you?

KLINGSOR

Ha! He who braves you, saves you as
  well:
so try out the lad, who draws near!

KUNDRY

I—will not!

KLINGSOR
(*who has mounted to the tower wall*)
So soon! He's climbing the wall.

KUNDRY

O sorrow! Sorrow!
Was this why you woke me?
Must I?—This?

KLINGSOR (*looking below*)
Ha! Quite a handsome youngster!

KUNDRY

Oh!—Oh!—Woe is me!

KLINGSOR (*blowing a horn*)
Ho! You watchmen! Ho! Warriors!
Heroes! Up! Foes are near!
Hey! How they rush to the ramparts,
the besotted vassals,
meaning to guard their beautiful devils!
So! Courage! Courage!
Ha—ha! He's quite without fear:
he took the sword from the valorous
  Ferris,
and with it he cuts his way through
  the swarm.
(*Kundry gives a gloomy, hysterical
  laugh.*)
The louts lack the ardor to cope with
  his zeal!
This—struck in the arm, that one—
  his thigh cut!
Ha-ha! They waver! They're fleeing!
Each campaigner runs home with his
  hurts!
You're welcome to all that!
Would that this crew,
this troublesome gang,
only might strangle each other!
Ha! How proudly he stands on the
  ramparts.
His count'nance is laughing and rosy,
he's gazing amazed
at the garden deserted so soon!
Hey, Kundry!
(*He turns around. Kundry has disap-
  peared; the bluish light has gone out,
  and deep darkness lies below.*)
How? Started work?
Ha-ha! I know the magic well,
which always will fetch you
whenever I wish!

(*He looks toward the garden.*)

You there! innocent sprout:
though your mission was foretold,

zu jung and dumm
fiel'st du in meine Gewalt:
die Reinheit dir entrissen,
bleibst mir du zugewiesen!

(*Er versinkt langsam mit dem ganzen
Turme; zugleich steigt der Zauber-
garten auf und erfüllt die Bühne
völlig. Tropische Vegetation, üp-
pigste Blumenpracht; nach dem Hintergrunde zu Abgrenzung durch die
Zinne der Burgmauer, an welche
sich seitwärts Vorsprünge des Schloss-
baues selbst (arabischen reichen
Styles) mit Terrassen anlehnen.*

*Auf der Mauer steht Parsifal, staunend
in den Garten hinabblickend.—Von
allen Seiten her, aus dem Garten wie
aus dem Palaste, stürzen, wirr durch
einander, einzeln, dann zugleich immer mehre, schöne Mädchen herein:
sie sind in flüchtig übergeworfener
Kleidung wie soeben aus dem Schlaf
aufgeschreckt.*)

MÄDCHEN
(*vom Garten kommend*)
Hier war das Tosen,
Waffen, wilde Rüfe!

MÄDCHEN
(*vom Schlosse heraus*)
Wehe! Rache! Auf!
Wo ist der Frevler?

EINZELNE
Mein Geliebter verwundet.

ANDERE
Wo find ich den Meinen?

ANDERE
Ich erwachte allein,
wohin entfloh er?

IMMER ANDERE
Drinnen im Saale!
Sie bluten! Wehe!
Wer ist der Feind?
Da steh't er! Seht!
Meines Ferris Schwert?
Ich sah's, er stürmte die Burg.
Ich hörte des Meisters Horn.
Mein Held lief herzu
sie Alle kamen, doch Jeden
empfing er mit blutiger Wehr.
Der Kühne! Der Feindliche!
Alle sie flohen ihm.
Du dort! Du dort!
Was schuf'st du uns solche Not?

Verwünscht, verwünscht sollst du sein!
(*Parsifal springt etwas tiefer in den
Garten herab.*)

DIE MÄDCHEN
Ha! Kühner! Wagst du zu trotzen?
Was schlug'st du uns're Geliebten?

PARSIFAL
Ihr schönen Kinder, musst' ich sie
nicht schlagen?
Zu euch ihr Holden ja wehrten sie
mir den Weg.

MÄDCHEN
Zu uns wolltest du?
Sah'st du uns schon?

PARSIFAL
Noch nie sah ich solch' zieres Ge-
schlecht:
nenn' ich euch schön, dünkt euch das
recht?

DIE MÄDCHEN
So willst du uns wohl nicht schlagen?

PARSIFAL
Das möcht ich nicht.

MÄDCHEN
Doch Schaden schuf'st du uns so vie-
len;
du schlugest uns're Gespielen!
Wer spielt nun mit uns?

PARSIFAL
Das tu' ich gern.

DIE MÄDCHEN
Bist du uns hold, so bleib' nicht fern;
und willst du uns nicht schelten,
wir werden dir's entgelten:
wir spielen nicht um Gold,
wir spielen um Minne's Sold.
Willst du auf Trost uns sinnen,
sollst den du uns abgewinnen!

(*Einzelne sind in die Lauben getreten,
und kommen jetzt, ganz wie in Blu-
mengewändern, selbst Blumen er-
scheinend, wieder zurück.*)

DIE GESCHMÜCKTEN MÄDCHEN
Lasset den Knaben! Er gehöret mir.
Nein! Nein! Mir! Mir!

DIE ANDERN MÄDCHEN
Ah, die Schlimmen! Sie schmückten
sich heimlich.

you're young and dumb,
and therefore fit for a fall:
your pur'ty once departed,
my power will make you serve me!

(*He and the tower sink quickly, and
at the same time the magic garden
emerges, with tropical vegetation and
luxurious flowers. In the background
is the battlemented castle, in elabo-
rate Arabic style. Parsifal is standing
on the wall, looking down on the
garden in amazement. Then from
garden and palace beautiful maidens
rush out, clad in filmy veils, which
seem to have been donned hastily,
as if their wearers had been suddenly
wakened from sleep.*)

MAIDENS

(*coming from the garden*)

Here was the tumult,
weapons, horrid outcries!

MAIDENS

(*coming from the castle*)

Sorrow! Vengeance! Up!
Who is the culprit?

ONE GROUP

My beloved is wounded.

ANOTHER

O, where is my sweetheart?

ANOTHER

When I woke, he had left me.
Where has he fled to?

OTHERS

Inside the castle?
They're bleeding! Horrors!
Who is the foe?
There! See him!
See, my Ferris' sword is in his hand!
I saw, he just stormed the walls.
I heard, too, the master's horn.
My knight ran this way;
they all of them rushed this way;
yet each was beat back by his might.
That bold one! That enemy!
All of them fled from him.
You there! You there!
Why have you caused us this woe!

Accursed, accursed may you be!
(*Parsifal leaps toward the garden. The
maidens start back.*)

MAIDENS

Dare you come near us?
Why have you injured our lovers?

PARSIFAL

You lovely children, should I not have
struck them?
They tried, fair maidens, to bar my
way from your bower.

MAIDENS

Were we what you sought?
Are we so fair?

PARSIFAL

Indeed, I've never witnessed such
grace.
Am I not right, calling you fair?

MAIDENS

You have no thought, then, to harm
us?

PARSIFAL

How could I have!

MAIDENS

You've done us
inj'ries, many inj'ries.
You badly injured our playmates!
Who'll play with us now?

PARSIFAL

I will—with joy!

MAIDENS

Be nice to us, and don't go far.
And if you do not chide us,
you'll gather love beside us.
We do not play for gold,
we play to let love unfold.
Would you like to console us,
then try to catch us and hold us!

(*Some, who had stepped out, return
now in floral dresses, looking very
much like flowers, and rush toward
Parsifal.*)

DECKED-OUT MAIDENS

Let go the youngster!—He belongs to
me.
No! No! Me! Me!

OTHER MAIDENS

Ah, how tricky! They went and
changed raiment!

DIE MÄDCHEN

Komm'! Komm'!
Holder Knabe!
Lass mich dir blühen!
Dir zu Wonn' und Labe
gilt mein minniges Mühen!

PARSIFAL

(*mit heit'rer Rube in der Mitte ste-
hend*)

Wie duftet ihr hold!
Seid ihr denn Blumen?

DIE MÄDCHEN

Des Gartens Zier
und duftende Geister
im Lenz pflückt uns der Meister;
wir wachsen hier
in Sommer und Sonne,
für dich erblühend in Wonne.
Nun sei uns freund und hold,
nicht karge den Blumen den Sold:
kannst du uns nicht lieben und minnen,
wir welken und sterben dahinnen.

ERSTES MÄDCHEN

An deinen Busen nimm mich!

ZWEITES

Die Stirn lass' mich dir kühlen!

DRITTES

Lass mich die Wange dir fühlen!

VIERTES

Den Mund lass' mich dir küssen!

FÜNFTES

Nein, mich! Die Schönste bin ich.

SECHSTES

Nein ich! Ich dufte süsser.

PARSIFAL

(*ihrer anmutigen Zudringlichkeit sanft
wehrend*)

Ihr wild holdes Blumengedränge,
soll ich mit euch spielen, entlasst mich
    der Enge!

MÄDCHEN

Was zankest du?

PARSIFAL

Weil ihr euch streitet.

MÄDCHEN

Wir streiten nur um dich.

PARSIFAL

Das meidet!

ERSTES MÄDCHEN

Du lass' von ihm: sieh', er will mich.

ZWEITES MÄDCHEN

Nein, mich!

DRITTES

Mich lieber!

VIERTES

Nein, mich!

ERSTES MÄDCHEN

Du wehrest mir?

ZWEITES

Scheuchest mich fort?

MÄDCHEN

Bist du feige vor Frauen?
Magst dich nicht getrauen?
Wie schlimm bist du Zager und Kalter!
Die Blumen lässt du umbuhlen den
    Falter?
Weichet dem Toren!
Ich geb' ihn verloren!
Uns sei er erkoren!
Nein, uns! Nein, mir!
Auch mir! Hier, hier!

PARSIFAL

Lass't ab! Ihr fangt mich nicht!

*Aus einem Blumenhage zur Seite ver-
nimmt man*

KUNDRY'S STIMME

Parsifal! Bleibe!

(*Die Mädchen erschrecken und halten
sogleich ein.—Parsifal steht betroffen
still.*)

PARSIFAL

Parsifal . . . ?
So nannte träumend mich einst die
    Mutter.

KUNDRY

Hier weile, Parsifal!
Dich grüsset Wonne und Heil zumal.
Ihr kindischen Buhlen, weichet von
    ihm:
früh welkende Blumen,
nicht euch ward er zum Spiele bestellt!
Geht heim, pflegt der Wunden:
einsam erharrt euch mancher Held.

DIE MÄDCHEN

(*zaghaft und widerstrebend sich von
    Parsifal entfernend*)

Dich zu lassen, dich zu meiden, —
O wehe! O wehe der Pein!
Von Allen möchten gern wir scheiden,

MAIDENS

Come! Come!
Gallant youngster,
I'll be your lover,
and then you'll discover
love each rapturous hour!

PARSIFAL (*standing among them*)

How sweetly you smell!
Are you then flowers?

MAIDENS

Our garden's pride
and pleasant aroma!
Our lord plucked us in springtime!
We flourish here
in sunlight of summer,
thus blooming for our newcomer.
Now be our sweetheart true,
begrudge not the flowers their due!
Sweetly must you love us and cherish,
or else we will wither and perish.

FIRST MAIDEN

Oh take me, love, to your heart!

SECOND MAIDEN

Your brow needs a cool blessing!

THIRD MAIDEN

Your cheeks were meant for caressing!

FOURTH MAIDEN

Your mouth asks me for kisses!

FIFTH MAIDEN

No! No! No! I am the fairest!

SIXTH MAIDEN

No! My smell is sweeter!

PARSIFAL

(*gently putting off their advances*)

You wild, lovely cluster of flowers,
if I join your frolic I must have more
    room here!

MAIDENS

Why do you chide?

PARSIFAL

Because you quarrel.

MAIDENS

We quarrel but for you.

PARSIFAL

Then stop it.

FIRST MAIDEN

Let him alone! See, he wants me!

SECOND MAIDEN

No, me!

THIRD MAIDEN

Me rather!

FOURTH MAIDEN

No, me!

FIRST MAIDEN

Avoiding me?

SECOND MAIDEN

You turn me away?

MAIDENS

Why of women so chary,
so fearful and wary?
How timid you are, and how prudish!
You'd have the butterflies wooed by the
    flowers?
How faint he is! How cold he is!
A blockhead, so let's leave him!
He's lost, so why receive him?
Why then let us retrieve him!
No, us! No, me!
And me! And me!

PARSIFAL

Let be! I'll not be caught!
(*He is about to flee when he hears
Kundry's voice and stands stone-
still. The maidens make an outcry.*)

KUNDRY

(*gradually coming into sight*)

Parsifal! Tarry!

PARSIFAL

Parsifal . . . ?
The name my mother once called me
while dreaming.

KUNDRY

Here tarry, Parsifal.
Now look for bliss and delight at once.
You frivolous wantons, leave him
    alone.
Fast-withering flowers,
who said he was to serve for your
    sport?
Go home, tend to your wounded!
Many neglected wait for your care.

MAIDENS

(*as they trembling and reluctantly
leave Parsifal*)

Must we leave you, must we part so?
Oh woe! Oh woe for the pain!
We'd gladly part from all companions

mit dir allein zu sein.
Leb' wohl! Leb' wohl!
Du Holder! Du Stolzer!
Du Tor!

(*Mit dem Letzten sind sie, unter leisem Gelächter, nach dem Schlosse zu verschwunden.*)

(*Parsifal sieht sich schüchtern nach der Seite hin um, von welcher die Stimme kam. Dort ist jetzt, durch Enthüllung des Hages, ein jugendliches Weib von höchster Schönheit—Kundry, in durchaus verwandelter Gestalt—auf einem Blumenlager, in leicht verhüllender, phantastischer Kleidung — annähernd arabischen Styles — sichtbar geworden.*)

PARSIFAL

Dies Alles—hab' ich nun geträumt?
Riefest du mich Namenlosen?

KUNDRY

Dich nannt' ich, tör'ger Reiner,
"Fal parsi", —
Dich, reinen Toren: "Parsifal".
So rief, da in arab'schem Land er verschied,
dein Vater Gamuret dem Sohne zu,
den er, im Mutterschooss verschlossen,
mit diesem Namen sterbend grüsste.
Dir ihn zu künden, harrt' ich deiner hier:
was zog dich her, wenn nicht der Kunde Wunsch?

PARSIFAL

Nie sah' ich, nie träumte mir, was jetzt ich schau', und was mit Bangen mich erfüllt.
Entblühtest du auch diesem Blumenhaine?

KUNDRY

Nein, Parsifal, du tör'ger Reiner!
Fern, fern, ist mein Heimat.
Dass du mich fändest, verweilte ich nur hier;
von weither kam ich, wo ich viel ersah'.
Ich sah das Kind an seiner Mutter Brust,
sein erstes Lallen lacht mir noch im Ohr:
das Leid im Herzen,
wie lachte da auch Herzeleide,
als ihren Schmerzen
zujauchzte ihrer Augen Weide!
Gebettet sanft auf weichen Moosen,
den hold geschläfert sie mit Kosen,

dem, bang' in Sorgen,
den Schlummer bewacht der Mutter Sehnen,
den weck't am Morgen
der heisse Tau der Mutter Tränen.
Nur Weinen war sie, Schmerz gebahren
um deines Vaters Lieb' und Tod;
vor gleicher Not dich zu bewahren,
galt ihr als höchster Pflicht Gebot.
Den Waffen fern, der Männer Kampf und Wüten,
wollte sie still dich bergen und behüten.
Nur Sorgen war sie, ach! und Bangen:
nie sollte Kunde zu dir hergelangen.
Hörst du nicht noch ihrer Klage Ruf,
wann spät und fern du geweilt?
Hei! Was ihr das Lust und Lachen schuf,
wann sie suchend dann dich ereilt;
wann dann ihr Arm dich wütend umschlang,
ward dir es wohl gar beim Küssen bang?
Doch ihr Wehe du nicht vernahm'st,
nicht ihrer Schmerzen Toben,
als endlich du nicht wieder kam'st,
und deine Spur verstoben.
Sie harrte Nächt' und Tage,
bis ihr verstummt die Klage,
der Gram ihr zehrte den Schmerz,
um stillen Tod sie warb:
ihr brach das Leid das Herz,
und Herzeleide starb.

PARSIFAL

Wehe! Wehe! Was tat ich? Wo war ich?
Mutter! Süsse, holde Mutter!
Dein Sohn, dein Sohn musste dich morden
O Tor! Blöder, taumelnder Tor!
Wo irrtest du hin, ihrer vergessend?
Deiner, deiner vergessend?
Traute, teuerste Mutter!

KUNDRY

War dir fremd noch der Schmerz,
des Trostes Süsse
labte nie auch dein Herz:
das Wehe, das dich reu't,
die Not nun büsse
im Trost, den Liebe beut!

PARSIFAL

Die Mutter, die Mutter konnt' ich vergessen!
Ha! Was Alles vergass ich wohl noch?
Wess' war ich je noch eingedenk?
Nur dumpfe Torheit lebt in mir!

to be alone with you.
Farewell! Farewell!
Most gracious! Most valiant!
Most—fool!

*(They disappear into the castle, laugh-
ing. Parsifal looks timidly in the di-
rection from which he heard the
voice. The branches of the arbor
separate and a young woman of sur-
passing beauty is seen: Kundry, quite
different from before. She is lying on
a flowery couch in diaphanous
drapery of somewhat Arabian
fashion.)*

PARSIFAL

Have I been in a dream just now?
Did you call me who am nameless?

KUNDRY

I called you, foolish pure one,
"Fal-parsi,"
Thus, pure and foolish: "Parsifal."
The name was uttered in far Araby's
land,
by Gamuret, your father, to that son
who still was locked within his mother;
and with this utt'rance death did take
him.
I've waited for you just to give this
news.
What drew you here, if not the wish
to know?

PARSIFAL

I've not seen, nor even dreamed, what
now
I see, and what with terror fills my
heart!
And did you too bloom in this flower
garden?

KUNDRY

No, Parsifal, you foolish virgin!
Far, far, the land I hale from.
I only tarried to be here when you
came.
And through this journey I have seen
a lot.
I saw the child upon its mother's
breast,
its cooing cries still linger in my ear.
Though filled with sorrow
she laughed through the tears of that
sorrow,
to hear the joy of her eyes
make cries of lovely laughter!
She gently made a mossy cradle;
it fell asleep from her caresses.

The anxious mother
protected its rest with sleepless vigil,
and in the morning
a mother's dewy tears awaked it.
Her face was tearful, sorrow's picture.
The cause: your father's love and
death.
She uttered ardent, holy prayers,
to save you from a fate like his.
Her dear desire was all to keep you
sheltered,
far from all arms, and mankind's war-
ring madness.
She loved you, watched you, and still
sorrowed:
all news of evil was kept from your
knowledge.
Do you not still hear her anguished cry,
when you tarried far from home?
Hey! How she rejoiced and laughed
that time
when she found you after her search,
and clutched her arms around you,
relieved,
what fear did you have of kisses then?
Yet you could not perceive her sorrow,
nor know that frenzied anguish.
And then at last you went for all time,
and left no trace behind you.
She waited for you daily,
until her woe was silenced,
till all was dull and dead.
She prayed for death to come,
then sorrow broke her heart,
and—Heart of Sorrow—died.

PARSIFAL

Sorrow! Sorrow! My misdeed? Where
was I?
Mother! Sweetest, dearest Mother!
Your son it was, your son that slew
you!
Oh fool! Blind and blundering fool!
Forgetful of you! Wandering wildly!
Forgetful, blindly forgetful!
Sweetest, dearest of mothers!

KUNDRY

Had you not harbored pain,
sweet consolation
could not visit your heart.
The woe that rends your soul
shall now give place to a joy
that springs from my love.

PARSIFAL

My mother, my mother! Could I forget
her?
Ha! Why is it I always forget?
Why don't I remember at all?
Just stupid folly lives in me!

KUNDRY

(*ihm den Arm um den Nacken schlingend*)

Bekenntniss
wird Schuld in Reue enden,
Erkenntniss
in Sinn die Torheit wenden.
Die Liebe lerne kennen,
die Gamuret umschloss,
als Herzeleid's Entbrennen
ihn sengend überfloss!
Die Leib und Leben
einst dir gegeben,
der Tod und Torheit weichen muss,
sie beut'
dir heut'—
als Muttersegens letzten Gruss
der Liebe ersten Kuss!

(*Sie hat ihr Haupt völlig über das seinige geneigt, und heftet nun ihre Lippen zu einem langen Kusse auf seinen Mund.*)

PARSIFAL

(*fährt plötzlich mit einer Gebärde des höchsten Schreckens anf: seine Haltung drückt eine furchtbare Veränderung aus: er stemmt seine Hände gewaltsam gegen sein Herz.*)

Amfortas!
Die Wunde! Die Wunde!
Sie brennt in meinem Herzen!
Oh, Klage! Klage!
Furchtbare Klage!
Aus tiefstem Herzen schreit sie mir auf.
Oh! Oh! Elender! Jammervollster!
Die Wunde seh' ich bluten:
nun blutet sie in mir!
Hier—Hier!

(*Während Kundry in Schrecken und Verwunderung auf ihn hinstarrt, fährt Parsifal in gänzlicher Entrücktheit fort.*)

Nein, nein! Nicht die Wunde ist es.
Fliesse ihr Blut in Strömen dahin!
Hier! Hier im Herzen der Brand!
Das Sehnen, das furchtbare Sehnen,
das alle Sinne mir fasst und zwingt!
Oh! Qual der Liebe!
Wie Alles schauert, bebt und zuckt
in sündigem Verlangen!
Es starrt der Blick dumpf auf das
    Heilsgefäss:
Das heil'ge Blut erglüht;
Erlösungswonne, göttlich mild',
durchzittert weithin alle Seelen;
nur hier, im Herzen, will die Qual nicht
    weichen.

Des Heiland's Klage da vernehm' ich,
die Klage, ach! die Klage
um das entweihte Heiligtum:
"Erlöse, rette mich
aus schuldbefleckten Händen!"
So rief die Gottesklage
furchtbar laut mir in die Seele.
Und ich? Der Tor, der Feige,
zu wilden Knabentaten floh' ich hin!
Erlöser! Heiland! Herr der Huld!
Wie büss' ich Sünder meine Schuld?

KUNDRY

(*deren Erstaunen in leidenschaftliche Bewunderung übergeht, sucht schüchtern sich Parsifal zu nähern*)

Gelobter Held! Entflieh dem Wahn!
Blick' auf! Sei hold der Huldin Nah'n!

PARSIFAL

(*immer in gebeugter Stellung, starr zu Kundry aufblickend, während diese sich zu ihm neigt und liebkosende Bewegungen ausführt*)

Ja! Diese Stimme! So rief sie ihm;
und diesen Blick, deutlich erkenn' ich
    ihn,
auch diesen, der ihm so friedlos lachte,
die Lippe, ja so zuckte sie ihm;
so neigte sich der Nacken,
so hob sich kühn das Haupt;
so flatterten lachend die Locken,
so schlang um den Hals sich der Arm,
so schmeichelte weich die Wange!
Mit aller Schmerzen Qual im Bunde,
    das Heil der Seele
entküsste ihm der Mund!
Ha! dieser Kuss!

(*Er stösst Kundry heftig von sich.*)

Verderberin! Weiche von mir!
Ewig, ewig von mir!

KUNDRY

Grausamer!
Fühlst du im Herzen,
nur And'rer Schmerzen,
so fühle jetzt auch die meinen!
Bist du Erlöser,
was bannt dich, Böser,
nicht mir auch zum Heil dich zu einen?
Seit Ewigkeiten harre ich deiner,
des Heiland's, ach! so spät,
den einst ich kühn geschmäht.
Oh! Kenntest du den Fluch,
der mich durch Schlaf und Wachen,
durch Tod und Leben, Pein und
    Lachen,
zu neuem Leiden neu gestählt,

KUNDRY

(*encircling his neck with her arm*)

Confession
makes guilt for errors vanish.
Admission
to self will folly banish.
Just learn to love in fashion
that Gamuret once loved,
when Heart of Sorrow's passion
his passion hotly moved.
And she who gave you
body and senses
must keep both death and folly far.
She sends by me
her final blessing and farewell:
she gives you love's—first kiss!

(*Bending completely over him, she plants a long kiss upon his lips. Parsifal starts up in terror, pressing his hand against his heart.*)

PARSIFAL

Amfortas!
The spear wound! The spear wound!
The pain burns in my bosom!
Oh sorrow! Sorrow!
Terrible torture!
A cry of anguish wells from my heart!
Wretched one!
Woeful suff'rer!
The wound has started bleeding!
I feel it bleed within.
Here, here!
No! No! Not the wound I thought it.
Let that outpour in streams if it will!
Here! Here! The brand in my heart!
The longing, the terrible longing,
that grips my senses in error's thrall!
Oh, love that torments!
How all within me thrills, and quakes
and throbs in sinful longing!

(*While Kundry stares in mingled fear and wonderment Parsifal appears to have fallen into a trance.*)

My glance is fixed fast on the healing cup,
the holy blood glows red.
Redemption's rapture, pure and mild,
sends healing power through creation.
But here, within me will the pain not lessen.

I hear the voice of our Redeemer,
ah, lamenting, lamenting
for the polluted sanctuary.
"Redeem me! Rescue me
from hands that guilt has tainted!"
So calls the voice from heaven,
fearful, loud, piercing my being.
And I, the fool, the craven,
to wild and childish actions hurry on!
Redeemer! Saviour! Lord of Grace!
How may a sinner blot such guilt?

KUNDRY

(*now passionately admiring, timidly approaches Parsifal*)

O valiant knight! Cast off this spell!
Look up! And love the one who loves!

PARSIFAL

(*staring blindly up at Kundry while she leans over him and caresses him*)

Ha! So she called him.
This was the voice, and this the look,—
clearly I know it well.
And this too, this was the smile she gave him.
The lips, too—yes, they quivered like that.
The neck was bent this manner,
the head was proudly raised.
Thus, laughing, she dangled her tresses,
and so put her arm round his neck.
His cheeks too she touched so gently,
and in league with mortal pain and error,
she kissed away the salvation of his soul!
Ha!—That dread kiss!
        (*He pushes Kundry away.*)
You sorceress! Out of my sight!
Leave me—forever—be gone!

KUNDRY

Dreadful one!
If you feel pain
in your heart for others,
then let me too share this pity!
If you're the Saviour,
what keeps you, bad one,
from granting the solace I ask for?
Through endless ages
I've waited your coming,
an advent, ah!—so late!—
of one I rashly spurned.
Oh, could you know the curse,
which through me, sleeping, waking,
in death or living,
pain and laughter,
—which meets new strength to front new foes—

endlos durch das dasein quält!
Ich sah Ihn—Ihn—
und—lachte . . .
da traf mich sein Blick.
Nun such' ich ihn von Welt zu Welt
ihm wieder zu begegnen.
In höchster Not
wähn' ich sein Auge schon nah',
den Blick schon auf mir ruh'n.
Da kehrt mir das verfluchte Lachen
  wieder,
ein Sünder sinkt mir in die Arme!
Da lach' ich—lache,
kann nicht weinen:
nur schreien, wüten,
toben, rasen
in stets erneu'ter Wahnsinn's Nacht,
aus der ich büssend kaum erwacht.
Den ich in Todesschmachten,
den ich erkannt, den blöd' Verlachten,
lass mich an seinem Busen weinen,
nur eine Stunde mich dir vereinen,
und ob mich Gott und Welt verstöss't,
in dir entsündigt sein und erlös't!

PARSIFAL

Auf Ewigkeit
wärst du verdammt mit mir
für eine Stunde
Vergessen's meiner Sendung
in deines Arm's Umfangen!
Auch dir bin ich zum Heil gesandt,
bleibst du dem Sehnen abgewandt.
Die Labung, die dein Leiden endet,
beut nicht der Quell, aus dem es fliesst,
das Heil wird nimmer dir gespendet,
eh' jener Quell sich dir nich schliesst.
Ein andres ist's,—ein andres, ach!
nach dem ich jammernd schmachten
  sah
die Brüder dort in grausen Nöten,
den Leib sich quälen und ertöten.
Doch wer erkennt ihn klar und hell,
des einz'gen Heiles wahren Quell?
Oh, Elend! Aller Rettung Flucht!
Oh, Weltenwahns Umnachten:
in höchsten Heiles heisser Sucht
nach der Verdammniss Quell zu
  schmachten!

KUNDRY

(in wilder Begeisterung)

So war es mein Kuss,
der welthellsichtig dich macht?
Mein volles Liebes Umfangen
lässt dich dann Gottheit erlangen.
Die Welt erlöse, ist dies dein Amt:
schuf dich zum Gott die Stunde,
für sie lass' mich ewig verdammt,
nie heile mir die Wunde.

PARSIFAL

Erlösung, Frevlerin, biet' ich auch dir.

KUNDRY

Lass' mich dich Göttlichen lieben,
Erlösung gabst du dann mir.

PARSIFAL

Lieb' und Erlösung soll dir werden,
zeigest du
zu Amfortas mir den Weg.

KUNDRY

Nie sollst du ihn finden!
Den Verfall'nen, lass' ihn verderben,
den Unseligen,
Schmach-lüsternen,
den ich verlachte—lachte—lachte!
Haha! Ihn traf ja der eig'ne Speer!

PARSIFAL

Wer durft' ihn verwunden mit heil'ger
  Wehr?

KUNDRY

Er—Er,
der einst mein Lachen bestraft:
sein Fluch—ha!—mir gibt er Kraft;
gegen dich selbst ruf' ich die Wehr,
gib'st du dem Sünder des Mitleid's
  Ehr!
Ha! Wahnsinn!
Mitleid! Mitleid mit mir!
Nur eine Stunde mein,
nur eine Stunde dein—:
und des Weges
sollst du geleitet sein!
(Sie will ihn umarmen. Er stösst sie
  heftig von sich.)

PARSIFAL

Vergeh', unseliges Weib!

KUNDRY

(zerschlägt sich die Brust, und ruft in
  wildem Rasen)

Hilfe! Hilfe! Herbei!
Haltet den Frechen! Herbei!
Wehr't ihm die Wege!
Wehr't ihm die Pfade!
Und flöhest du von hier, und fändest
all Wege der Welt,
den Weg, den du suchst,
dess' Pfade sollst du nicht finden!
Denn Pfad und Wege,
die dich mir entführen,
so verwünsch' ich sie dir:
Irre! Irre,
mir so vertraut!
Dich weih' ich ihm zum Geleit'!

gives my being endless woe!
I saw Him—Him—
and—mocked Him—
I felt then—His look:
I seek Him now from world to world.
Again I hope to meet him.
I feel His eye near, in the time of my
need.
His glance rests on me now.
Yet from me—comes again this cursed
laughter!
A sinner sinks in my embraces!
Just laughter moves me, for tears cannot;
just shouting, raging,
fuming, raving,
cloud upon cloud from error's night,
from which, repentant, scarce I've
waked.
In mortal shame I waited sadly
the one that I rejected madly.
So let me weep upon your bosom,
and give me solace, an hour's a-tone-
ment,
and though I'm spurned by God and
man,
my soul will be redeemed, and at
peace.

PARSIFAL

A full damnation
both of us would share
for such atonement,
if I forgot my mission
within your arms' embraces!
Yet I was sent to heal you too,
if you put off your wrong desire.
The solace which will end your sorrow
does not arise from error's source;
and never will you gain your healing
until you stop the source of sin.
Far otherwise, far diff'rent, ah,
for me to see that grievous sight—
the Brothers there, in direful need,
with their bodies wasting, lost in anguish.
But who has such unclouded sight
to know the truth that makes man
free?
Oh, wretched, where is counsel gone?
Oh, dreadful night of error,
to seek with zeal the source of good,
though it's perdition's chains you pine
for!

KUNDRY (*in wild ecstasy*)

So was it my kiss
that gave this all-seeing vision?
Then let my loving embraces
give you the Godhood you look for!

The world's redemption, is this your
charge?
It's God who made this moment,
for it let me perish evermore,
my wound unhealed forever!

PARSIFAL

Redemption, wanton one, take of it
now.

KUNDRY

Let me, divine one, then love you.
Salvation such as that I want.

PARSIFAL

Love and redemption I can offer
If the way to Amfortas is revealed.

KUNDRY

No! Never shall you find him!
Leave that lost one, and let him perish,
so unholy, vile, lecherous,
fit but for laughter, laughter, laughter,
ha-ha!
He fell by the spear that he owned!

PARSIFAL

Who dared, though, to wound him
with that holy spear?

KUNDRY

He—He!
Who gave me reason to laugh.
His curse, ha, it gives me strength.
Against you too I turn the spear,
since you show pity where none is due!
Ha! Madness! Pity? Pity for me?
Were you just one hour mine!
Were I just one hour yours!
And then, after, I would reveal the
path.

PARSIFAL

Away, iniquitous wretch!
(*She tries to embrace him, but he re-
pulses her violently. She becomes
furious and makes an outcry.*)

KUNDRY

Help me! This way! Oh, help!
Stop the marauder! Come here!
Guard all the ways there.
Bar every roadway!
And though you flee from here,
and seek through all the ways of the
world,
one road which you seek,
one road you shall find—never:
that path and highway which leads you
from my presence.
Thus, I curse them for you!
Wander! Wander! Back you will come!
Here is the guide that you need!

(*Klingsor ist auf der Burgmauer heraus
getreten; die Mädchen stürzen ebenfalls aus dem Schlosse und wollen
auf Kundry zueilen.*)

KLINGSOR
(*eine Lanze schwingend*)

Halt da! dich bann' ich mit der rechten
Wehr:
den Toren stelle mir seines Meisters
Speer!

(*Er schleudert auf Parsifal den Speer,
welcher über dessen Haupte schwe-
ben bleibt; Parsifal erfasst ihn mit
der Hand und schwingt ihn, mit
einer Gebärde höchster Entzückung,
die Gestalt des Kreuzes bezeich-
nend.*)

PARSIFAL

Mit diesem Zeichen bann' ich deinen
Zauber:
wie die Wunde er schliesse,
die mit ihm du schlugest,
in Trauer und Trümmer
stürz er die trügende Pracht!

(*Wie durch ein Erdbeben versinkt das
Schloss; der Garten verdorrt zur
Einöde; die Mädchen liegen als ver-
welkte Blumen am Boden umher
gestreut.—Kundry ist schreiend zusammen gesunken.*)

Du weisst —
wo du mich wieder finden kannst!

(*Er verschwindet. Der Vorhang schliesst
sich schnell.*)

DRITTER AUGZUG

IM GEBIETE DES GRALES

*Freie, anmutige Frühlingsgegend mit
nach dem Hintergrunde zu sanft
ansteigender Blumenaue. Den Vor-
dergrund nimmt der Saum des Waldes ein, der sich nach rechts zu aus-
dehnt. Im Vordergrunde, an der
Waldseite, ein Quell; ihm gegenüber,
etwas tiefer, eine schlichte Einsiedler-
hütte, an einen Felsen gelehnt. Früh-
ester Morgen.*

*Gurnemanz, zum hohen Greise gealtert,
als Einsiedler, nur in das Hemd des
Gralsritters dürftig gekleidet tritt aus
der Hütte und lauscht.*

GURNEMANZ

Von dorther kam das Stöhnen.
So jammervoll klagt kein Wild,
und gewiss gar nicht am heiligsten
Morgen heut'.
Mich dünkt, ich kenne diesen Klage-
ruf?

(*Ein dumpfes Stöhnen, wie von einer
im tiefen Schlafe durch Träume
Geängstigten, wird vernommen.—
Gurnemanz schreitet entschlossen
einer Dornenhecke auf der Seite zu:
diese ist gänzlich überwachsen: er
reisst mit Gewalt das Gestrüpp aus-
einander: dann hält er plötzlich an.*)

Ha! Sie wieder da?
Das winterlich rauhe Gedörn'
hielt sie verdeckt: wie lang' schon?
Auf! Kundry! Auf!
Der Winter floh, und Lenz ist da!
Erwach,' erwache dem Lenz!
Kalt und starr!
Diesmal hielt' ich sie wohl für tot:
doch war's ihr Stöhnen, was ich ver-
nahm?

(*Er zieht Kundry, ganz erstarrt und
leblos, aus dem Gebüsche hervor,
trägt sie auf einen nahen Rasenhügel, reibt ihr stark die Hände und
Schläfe, haucht sie an und bemüht
sich in Allem, um die Erstarrung
weichen zu machen. Endlich erwacht
sie. Sie ist, gänzlich wie im ersten
Aufzuge, im wilden Gewande der
Gralsbotin; nur ist ihre Gesichtsfarbe
bleicher, aus Miene und Haltung ist
die Wildheit gewichen. Sie starrt
lange Gurnemanz an. Dann erhebt
sie sich, ordnet sich Kleidung und
Haar, und geht sofort wie eine Magd
an die Bedienung.*)

GURNEMANZ

Du tolles Weib!
Hast du kein Wort für mich?
Ist dies der Dank,
dass dem Todesschlafe
noch einmal ich dich entweckt?

KUNDRY
(*neigt langsam das Haupt; dann bringt
sie, rauh und abgebrochen, hervor*):
Dienen, dienen!

GURNEMANZ
(*schüttelt den Kopf*)
Das wird dich wenig müh'n!
Auf Botschaft sendet sich's nicht mehr:

(Klingsor has stepped out on the castle wall and aimed the lance at Parsifal.)

KLINGSOR

Halt there! This weapon serves to bar
  your way!
The holy fool shall now meet his
  master's spear.

(He hurls the lance, but it stops suspended in air over Parsifal's head. Parsifal seizes it and holds it over his head.)

PARSIFAL

With this blest sign I banish all your
  magic.
As the spear that has wounded
shall be used for healing,
so let this destruction
fall on illusory pomp.

(He makes the sign of the cross. The castle is swallowed up, the garden becomes a wilderness, and Kundry, shrieking, sinks to the ground. Parsifal hurries away but turns again to Kundry, when he reaches the top of the ruined wall.)

You know
where you can find me once again.

(As he leaves, Kundry raises her head and stares after him.)

ACT III

A pleasant landscape in the domain of the Grail. A flowery meadow whose foreground is occupied by the edge of a forest that stretches out over a rocky ascent toward the right. Near the edge of the woods is a spring opposite to which, a little farther back, can be seen the simple hut of a hermit, built against a rock. It is very early morning.

(Gurnemanz, greatly aged, clad as a hermit in the tunic of a knight of the Grail, steps out of the hut and listens.)

GURNEMANZ

From over there the moans came.
No beast would make sounds like that
—and the least upon this holiest day
  on earth.

(Kundry's voice is heard in low groans.)

I think I know that sad, complaining
  cry.

(He walks toward a thicket of thorns. He pulls the dense bushes forcibly apart, then stops suddenly.)

Ha! She here again?
Discourteous, wintery thorns kept her
  concealed.
How long now?
Up! Kundry! Up!
The winter's fled, and spring has come!

(He draws Kundry, stiff and lifeless, from the bushes and carries her to a grassy mound nearby.)

Awaken, awake to the spring!
Cold—and stiff!
This time really I thought her dead:
Yet was it not her groans that I heard?

(He rubs her hands and temples. Finally she opens her eyes, then shrieks. How different she is! She is clad in the coarse garb of a penitent, as in the first act, but her complexion is paler. She has lost her wildness. She stares long at Gurnemanz, then she arises, arranges her clothing and hair, and appears ready to serve the Knights.)

You harebrained wench,
have you no word for me?
Is this the thanks
that I get
for breaking
your deathlike sleep once again?

KUNDRY

(slowly bows her head, then cries brokenly and hoarsely)

Service! Service!

GURNEMANZ

(shaking his head)

There's little toil for you:
We have no errands any more.

Kräuter und Wurzeln
findet ein Jeder sich selbst,
wir lernen's im Walde vom Tier.

(*Kundry hat sich während dem um-
gesehen, gewahrt die Hütte, und
geht hinein.*)

GURNEMANZ

(*verwundert ihr nachblickend*)

Wie anders schreitet sie als sonst!
Wirkte das der heilige Tag?
Oh! Tag der Gnade ohne Gleichen!
Gewiss, zu ihrem Heile
durft' ich der Armen heut'
den Todesschlaf verscheuchen.

(*Kundry kommt wieder aus der Hütte;
sie trägt einen Wasserkrug und geht
damit zum Quelle. Während sie auf
die Füllung wartet, blickt sie in den
Wald, und bemerkt dort in der Ferne
einen Kommenden; sie wendet sich
zu Gurnemanz, um ihn darauf hinzu-
deuten.*)

Wer nahet dort dem heiligen Quell?
In düst'ren Waffenschmucke?
Das ist der Brüder keiner.

(*Kundry entfernt sich mit dem ge-
füllten Kruge langsam nach der
Hütte, in welcher sie sich zu schaffen
macht. Gurnemanz tritt staunend bei
Seite, um den Ankommenden zu beo-
bachten. Parsifal tritt aus dem Walde
auf. Er ist ganz in schwarzer Waffen-
rüstung: mit geschlossenem Helme
und gesenktem Speer, schreitet er,
gebeugten Hauptes, träumerisch zö-
gernd, langsam daher, und setzt sich
auf dem kleinen Rasenhügel am
Quelle nieder.*)

GURNEMANZ

(*betrachtet ihn lange, und tritt dann
etwas näher*)

Heil dir, mein Gast!
Bist du verirrt, und soll ich dich wei-
sen?

(*Parsifal schüttelt sanft das Haupt.*)

Entbietest du mir keinen Gruss?

(*Parsifal neigt das Haupt.*)

Hei! Was?
Wenn dein Gelübde
dich bindet mir zu schweigen,
so mahnt das meine mich,
dass ich dir sage, was sich ziemt.
Hier bist du an geweihtem Ort:
da zieht man nicht mit Waffen her,
geschloss'nen Helmes, Schild und Speer.

Und heute gar! Weisst du denn nicht,
welch' heil'ger Tag heut' ist?

(*Parsifal schüttelt mit dem Kopfe.*)

Ja! Woher kommst du denn?
Bei welchen Heiden weiltest du,
zu wissen nicht, dass heute
der allerheilgste Char-Freitag ist?

(*Parsifal senkt das Haupt noch tiefer.*)

Schnell ab die Waffen!
Kränke nicht den Herrn, der heute,
baar jeder Wehr, sein heilig Blut
der sündigen Welt zur Sühne bot!

(*Parsifal erhebt sich, nach einem aber-
maligen Schweigen, stösst den Speer
vor sich in den Boden, legt Schild
und Schwert davor nieder, öffnet den
Helm, nimmt ihn vom Haupte und
legt ihn zu den anderen Waffen,
worauf er dann zu stummem Gebete
vor dem Speer niederkniet. Gurnemanz betrachtet ihn mit Erstaunen
und Rührung. Er winkt Kundry herbei, welche soeben aus der Hütte
getreten ist. Parsifal erhebt jetzt in
brünstigem Gebete seinen Blick an-
dachtvoll zu der Lanzenspitze auf.*)

GURNEMANZ

(*leise zu Kundry*)

Erkenn'st du ihn?
Der ist's, der einst den Schwan erlegt.

(*Kundry bestätigt mit einem leisen
Kopfnicken.*)

Gewiss 's ist Er!
Der Tor, den ich zürnend von uns
wies.
Ha! Welche Pfade fand er?
Der Speer, ich kenne ihn.
Oh! Heiligster Tag,
an dem ich heut' erwachen sollt'!

PARSIFAL

(*erhebt sich langsam vom Gebete,
blickt ruhig um sich, erkennt Gurnemanz, und reicht diesem sanft die
Hand zum Gruss*)

Heil mir, dass ich dich wieder finde!

GURNEMANZ

So kennst auch du mich noch?
Erkenn'st mich wieder,
den Gram und Not so tief gebeugt?
Wie kam'st du heut woher?

PARSIFAL

Der Irrniss und der Leiden Pfade kam
ich;

Herbs and simples
everyone finds for himself.
The beasts of the forest showed how.

(*Kundry enters the hut, to Gurnemanz's surprise.*)

How changed her step from what it
   was.
Did the holy day bring the change?
O day of grace without an equal!
Thank God, I was allowed
to banish the wretch's
deathlike sleep, for her salvation.

(*She comes out of the hut, carrying a
pitcher, which she takes to the
spring. Looking toward the forest,
she sees something and calls Gurnemanz's attention to the fact.*)

Who comes here toward the holy
   spring?

(*She disappears into the hut again to
work. At the same moment Parsifal
enters.*)

Those somber, warlike trappings?
I see it's not a Brother.

(*Head bowed low, Parsifal advances
dreamily, hesitatingly, then seats
himself on the grassy mound by the
spring. He is in black armor, with
closed visor. He sets down his spear.
Gurnemanz, having gazed long at
Parsifal in astonishment, now approaches him.*)

Greetings, Sir Guest!
Did you get lost, and shall I direct
   you?

(*Parsifal merely shakes his head.*)

You offer no greeting to me?

(*Parsifal bows his head.*)

Hey! What?
If you are bound by a solemn vow of
   silence,
I have a duty too: that I should tell
   you what is meet.
The present place is holy ground.
No man comes here with arms of war,
with visored helmet, shield and spear.

And least today!
Do you not know what holy day this is?

(*Parsifal shakes his head.*)

Well! From where have you come?
Among what pagans have you lived,
   not to know
that this is the ever-holiest Good Friday morn?
(*Parsifal sinks his head still lower.*)
Off with your weapons!
Injure not the Lord, who on this day
   shed His blood,
and not resisting evil, redeemed most
   sinful man!

(*After a further moment of silence
Parsifal rises, thrusts his spear into
the ground, lays shield and sword
beside it, raises his visor, takes the
helmet from his head, and places it
beside the other weapons. He kneels
in silent prayer before the spear.
Gurnemanz watches him with wonder and emotion. Then he beckons
to Kundry, who has just returned
from the hut.*)

GURNEMANZ
(*softly to Kundry*)

D'you know this man?
It's he who once laid low our swan!
   (*Kundry nods.*)
Indeed, it's he, the fool, whom I rough-
   ly turned away.
Ha! Yet he found the pathway?
I know that spear of his.
Oh, holiest day, to which my soul
   awakes with joy!

PARSIFAL

(*rises slowly, looks calmly about, recognizes Gurnemanz, and extends his
hand to him in kindly greeting*)

Thank God that I again have found
   you.

GURNEMANZ

Then do you know me still,
the patient Brother, whose frame is
   bent from grief and care?
How come you here, and whence?

PARSIFAL

My errors and the path of sorrow
   brought me.

soll ich mich denen jetzt entwunden
    wähnen,
da dieses Waldes Rauschen
wieder ich vernehme,
dich guten greisen neu begrüsse?
Oder irr' ich wieder?
Verändert dünkt mich Alles.

GURNEMANZ
So sag', zu wem den Weg du suchtest?

PARSIFAL
Zu ihm, dess' tiefe Klagen
ich törig staunend einst vernahm,
dem nun ich Heil zu bringen
mich auserlesen wähnen darf.
Doch—ach!
den Weg des Heiles nie zu finden,
in pfadlosen Irren
trieb ein wilder Fluch mich umher:
zahllose Nöte,
Kämpfe und Streite
zwangen mich ab vom Pfade,
wähnt' ich ihn recht schon erkannt.
Da musste mich Verzweiflung fassen,
das Heiltum heil mir zu bergen,
um das zu hüten, das zu wahren,
ich Wunden jeder Wehr' mir gewann.
Denn nicht ihn selber
durft' ich führen im Streite,
unentweih't führ' ich ihn mir zur Seite,
den nun ich heim geleite,
der dort dir schimmert heil und hehr:
des Grales heil'gen Speer.

GURNEMANZ
O Gnade! Höchstes Heil!
O Wunder! Heilig hehrstes Wunder!
O Herr! War es ein Fluch,
der dich vom rechten Pfad vertrieb,
so glaub', er ist gewichen.
Hier bist du, dies des Gral's Gebiet,
dein' harret seine Ritterschaft.
Ach, sie bedarf des Heiles,
des Heiles, das du bring'st!
Seit dem Tage, den du hier geweilt,
die Trauer, so da kund dir ward,
das Bangen wuchs zur höchsten Not.
Amfortas, gegen seiner Wunden,
seiner Seele Qual sich wehrend,
begehrt' in wütendem Trotze nun den
    Tod.
Kein Fleh'n, kein Elend seiner Ritter
bewog ihn mehr des heil'gen Amt's zu
    walten.
Im Schrein verschlossen bleibt seit lang'
    der Gral:
so hofft sein sündenreu'ger Hüter,
da er nicht sterben kann,

wann je er ihn erschaut,
sein Ende zu erzwingen,
und mit dem Leben seine Qual zu
    enden.
Die heil'ge Speisung bleibt uns nun
    versagt,
gemeine Atzung muss uns nähren:
darob versiegte unsrer Helden Kraft.
Nie kommt uns Botschaft mehr,
noch Ruf zu heil'gen Kämpfen aus der
    Ferne;
bleich und elend wankt umher
die mut- und führerlose Ritterschaft.
Hier in der Waldeck' barg ich selber
    mich,
des Todes still gewärtig,
dem schon mein alter Waffenherr ver-
    fiel;
denn Titurel, mein heil'ger Held,
den nun des Grales Anblick nicht mehr
    labte,
er starb, ein Mensch, wie Alle!

PARSIFAL
(vor grossem Schmerz sich aufbäu-
mend)
Und ich, ich bin's,
der all' dies Elend schuf!
Ha! Welcher Sünden,
welchel's Freves Schuld
muss dieses Toren Haupt
seit Ewigkeit belasten,
da keine Busse, keine Sühne
der Blindheit mich entwindet,
zur Rettung selbst ich auserkoren,
in Irrniss wild verloren,
der Rettung letzter Pfad mir schwin-
det!

(Er droht ohnmächtig umzusinken.
Gurnemanz hält in aufrecht, und
senkt ihn zum Sitze auf den Rasenhügel nieder. Kundry hat ein Becken
mit Wasser herbeigeholt, um Parsifal
zu besprengen.)

GURNEMANZ
Nicht so!
Die heil'ge Quelle selbst
erquicke uns'res Pilgers Bad.
Mir ahnt, ein hohes Werk
hab' er noch heut' zu wirken,
zu walten eines heil'gen Amtes:
so sei er fleckenrein,
und langer Irrfahrt Staub
soll jetzt von ihm gewaschen sein.

(Parsifal wird von den Beiden sanft zum
Rande des Quelles gewendet. Während Kundry ihm die Beinschienen
löst und dann die Füsse badet, Gur-

Yet let me fancy my trials are over,
since I can hear the sweetly sounding
    forest murmurs.
And is it you, good sage, who greet me,
or else—further error?
For all things here seem diff'rent.

GURNEMANZ

Now say just who it is you look for.

PARSIFAL

For him I heard lamenting,
and listened awe-struck, like a fool!
I think perhaps that I have been sent
to heal him of his woes.
But ah, I never found the path of
    healing.
I wandered in error, so enforced by a
    clinging curse.
Numberless troubles, battles and con-
    flicts,
forced me to leave the pathway,
just when I thought myself right.
Then did a desperation seize me
to keep the spear in concealment
and thus protect it from all hazard.
I gathered wounds from every fray
because in conflict never once did I
    wear it.
Unprofaned at my side now I bear it,
so home and knights may share it.
You see it shimm'ring, pure and clear:
the Grail's most holy spear!

GURNEMANZ

O glorious healing grace!
O wonder! Holy, lofty wonder!
Dear lord,
if 'twas a curse that kept you from the
    proper path,
be sure that curse is ended.
Here are you in the Grail's domain,
the noble band awaits you still.
Ah, they have need of healing, the
    healing that you bring!
Since that sojourn, when you tarried
    here,
the mourning which you witnessed
    then,
the sorrow, greatly has increased.
Amfortas, fighting with his suff'ring,
racked with pain of soul and body,
at last in raging defiance craved for
    death.
Beseechings, nor outcries of his knight-
    hood
could move him any more to serve the
    chalice,
and long it rested, hidden in the shrine.
Its guardian, sinful but repentant,

because he could not die while looking
    on the Grail,
would force his own quietus,
and end his life and all his pains to-
    gether.
Our holy manna thus is quite denied .
We're nourished now with common
    viands
and so our valor all has passed away.
No message ever comes,
nor call to holy warfare from far
    countries.
Pale and wretched, now,
our knights do mope,
they're lacking both a lord and heart!
I've sought seclusion
here within these woods,
and wait that death in silence,
which has already called my lord at
    arms:
for Titurel, my holy lord,
at last no more enjoyed the holy vessel
and died, a man, and mortal!

PARSIFAL

(*springing up in intense grief*)

And I am he, the cause of all this woe!
Ha! What transgressions, what out-
    rageous guilt
must this mad, foolish head
be evermore bemoaning!
Since no repentance, no atonement
can wash away my blindness!
To point the pathway I was chosen,
but now I'm lost in error,
and so myself I need that pathway.

(*He is about to fall in a faint. Gurnemanz sustains him and seats him on
the mound. Kundry hastens to bring
a basin of water to revive him. She
returns.*)

GURNEMANZ

Not yet!
But let the holy spring itself refresh
    the pilgrim's bath.
I sense a mighty work remains to do
    this morning,
to mind the Grail in holy service.
He must be free from stain, so let the
    trav'ler's dust
that spots him fast be washed away.

(*The two gently turn Parsifal toward
the spring. During what follows*)

*nemanz ihm aber den Brustharnisch
entnimmt, frägt)*

PARSIFAL

Werd' heut' ich zu Amfortas noch geleitet?

GURNEMANZ

Gewisslich; uns'rer harrt die hehre
Burg:
die Totenfeier meines lieben Herrn,
sie ruft mich selbst dahin.
Den Gral noch einmal uns da zu ent-
hüllen,
des lang' versäumten Amtes
noch einmal heut' zu walten,
zur Heiligung des hehren Vaters,
der seines Sohnes Schuld erlag,
die der nun also büssen will,
gelobt' Amfortas uns.

PARSIFAL

*(mit Verwunderung Kundry zuseh-
end)*

Du wuschest mir die Füsse,
nun netze mir das Haupt der Freund.

GURNEMANZ

*(mit der Hand aus dem Quell schöp-
fend und Parsifal's Haupt bespreng-
end)*

Gesegnet sei, du Reiner, durch das
Reine!
So weiche jeder Schuld
Bekümmerniss von dir!

*(Während dem hat Kundry ein golde-
nes Fläschchen aus dem Busen ge-
zogen, und von seinem Inhalte auf
Parsifal's Füsse ausgegossen; jetzt
trocknet sie diese mit ihren schnell
aufgelösten Haaren.)*

PARSIFAL

Du salbtest mir die Füsse,
das Haupt nun salbe Titurel's Genoss,
dass heute noch als König er mich
grüsse.

GURNEMANZ

*(schüttet das Fläschchen vollends auf
Parsifal's Haupt aus, reibt dieses
sanft, und faltet dann die Hände
darüber)*

So ward es uns verhiessen,
so segne ich dein Haupt,
als König dich zu grüssen.
Du Reiner.
Mitleidvoll Duldender,
heiltatvoll Wissender!

Wie des Erlös'ten Leiden du gelitten,
die letzte Last entnimm nun seinem
Haupt.

PARSIFAL

*(schöpft unvermerkt Wasser aus der
Quelle, neigt sich zu der vor ihm
noch knienden Kundry, und netzt
ihr das Haupt)*

Mein erstes Amt verricht' ich so:
die Taufe nimm,
und glaub' an den Erlöser!

*(Kundry senkt das Haupt tief zur Erde
und scheint heftig zu weinen. Parsifal wendet sich um, und blickt mit
sanfter Entzückung auf Wald und
Wiese.)*

Wie dünkt mich doch die Aue heut'
so schön!
Wohl traf ich Wunderblumen an,
die bis zum Haupte süchtig mich um-
rankten;
doch sah' ich nie so mild und zart
die Halme, Blüten und Blumen,
noch duftete All' so kindisch hold
und sprach so lieblich traut zu mir.

GURNEMANZ

Das ist Charfreitags Zauber, Herr!

PARSIFAL

O Wehe, des höchsten Schmerzentag's!
Da sollte, wähn' ich, was da blüh't
was atmet, lebt und wieder lebt,
nur trauern, ach! und weinen.

GURNEMANZ

Du sieh'st, das ist nicht so.
Des Sünders Reuetränen sind es,
die heut' mit heil'gem Tau
beträufet Flur und Au':
der liess sie so gedeihen.
Nun freu't sich alle Kreatur,
auf des Erlösers holder Spur,
will ihr Gebet ihm weihen.
Ihn selbst am Kreuze kann sie nicht
erschauen:
da blickt sie zum erlös'ten Menschen
auf;
der fühlt sich frei von Sündenlast und
Grauen,
durch Gottes Liebesopfer rein und
heil:
das merkt nun Halm und Blume auf
den Auen,
dass heut' des Menschen Fuss sie nicht
zertritt,
doch wohl, wie Gott mit himmlischer
Geduld

Kundry loosens his greaves; Gurne-
manz removes his breastplate.)

PARSIFAL

Do you mean to lead me now to Amfortas?

GURNEMANZ

Most surely! For the noble court
awaits.
The funeral service of my dearest lord
now summons me within.
For us the Grail must be once more
uncovered,
whose long-neglected service once more
must be attended,
to sanctify that noble father,
who by his son's great guilt was slain,
for which the son would now atone.
Amfortas made this vow.

(*Kundry, with humble zeal, bathes*
Parsifal's feet; he gazes on her with
silent wonderment.)

PARSIFAL

You've washed my feet with water, so
sprinkle now my head, my friend.

(*Gurnemanz takes water and does so.*)

GURNEMANZ

May you be blessed, O pure one,
through your pur'ty!
Forevermore may you be free from
guilt and care!

(*While Gurnemanz is performing this*
ceremony Kundry takes a gold flask
from her bosom and pours some of
the contents over Parsifal's feet, dry-
ing them with her hair, which she
has hastily unbound. Parsifal gently
takes the flask from Kundry and
passes it to Gurnemanz.)

PARSIFAL

You laved my feet, and thank you.

(*to Gurnemanz*)

Anoint my head, O friend of Titurel,
that so as king I may be greeted!

GURNEMANZ

(*pours the remainder of the contents*
of the flask on Parsifal's head and
places his hands on it in blessing)

Thus was it all predicted!
My blessing on your head:
I greet you as our master!
O pure one!
Patient and pitying one, healing and
knowing one!

As the Redeemer suffered, you have
suffered.
Remove the last of burdens from his
head!

PARSIFAL

(*has quietly taken some water from*
the spring in his hands, and now he
bends over Kundry, who is kneeling
before him and pours it over her
head)

I thus perform my first of tasks:
be now baptized,
believe in the Redeemer!

(*Kundry sinks her head to the ground*
and appears to weep passionately.
Parsifal turns about and with gentle
ecstasy gazes upon woods and mead-
ows now bathed in the light of
morning.)

How beautiful the meadows seem today!
Well I recall the wondrous flowers
which once did try to twine themselves
around me.
Yet they did not compare with these.
The grasses, blossoms and flowers
are fragrant in their innocence,
and speak to me with loving trust.

GURNEMANZ

That is Good Friday's magic, lord!

PARSIFAL

O sorrow, that day of greatest grief,
When all that's living, all that breathes
and blossoms,
living once again,
should only weep and sorrow!

GURNEMANZ

You see, it is not so.
The tears of sorrow wept by sinners
today have sprinkled field and plain
with holy dew,
which thereby consecrates them.
Today all living things rejoice
to see the signs of God's dear grace,
and with their thoughts they praise
Him.
The cross is lofty, so they cannot view
it.
But still their gaze can reach to man
redeemed,
who feels himself set free from sin and
sorrow,
by Love's great power made both pure
and whole.
The grass knows well, and flower of
the meadow,
today the foot of man can do no harm;
for just as God reveals to man

sich sein' erbarmt' und für ihn litt,
der Mensch auch heut' in frommer
  Huld
sie schont mit sanftem Schritt.
Das dankt dann alle Kreatur,
was all' da blüht und bald erstirbt,
da die entsündigte Natur
heut' ihren Unschuldstag erwirbt.

(*Kundry hat langsam wieder das
Haupt erhoben, und blickt, feuchten
Auges, ernst und ruhig bittend zu
Parsifal auf.*)

PARSIFAL

Ich sah' sie welken, die mir lachten:
ob heut' sie nach Erlösung schmachten?
Auch deine Träne wird zum Segens-
  taue:
du weinest, sieh', es lacht die Aue!

(*Er küsst sie sanft auf die Stirne.*)

(*Fernes Glockengeläute, sehr allmählich anschwellend.*)

GURNEMANZ

Mittag:
Die Stund' ist da.
Gestatte, Herr, dass dich dein Knecht
  geleite!

(*Gurnemanz hat Waffenrock und
Mantel des Gralsritters herbeigeholt;
er und Kundry bekleiden Parsifal
damit. Die Gegend verwandelt sich
sehr allmählich, ähnlicher Weise wie
im ersten Aufzuge, nur von rechts
nach links. Parsifal ergreift feierlich
den Speer und folgt mit Kundry
langsam dem geleitenden Gurnemanz.—Nachdem der Wald gänzlich
verschwunden ist, und Felsentore
sich aufgetan haben, in welchen die
Drei unsichtbar geworden sind, gewahrt man, bei fortdauerend an-
wachsendem Geläute, in gewölbten
Gangen Züge von Rittern in Trau-
ergewändern. — Endlich stellt sich
der ganze grosse Saal, wie im ersten
Aufzuge (nur ohne die Speisetafeln)
wieder dar. Düstere Beleuchtung.
Die Türen öffnen sich wieder. Von
einer Seite ziehen die Ritter, Titurel's
Leiche im Sarge geleitend, herein.
Auf der andern Seite wird Amfortas
im Siechbette, vor ihm der verhüllte
Schrein mit dem "Grale", getragen.
In der Mitte ist der Katafalk errich-
tet, dahinter der Hochsitz mit dem*
Baldachin, auf welchen Amfortas
wieder niedergelassen wird.*)

ERSTER ZUG

Geleiten wir im bergenden Schrein
den Gral zum heiligen Amte,
wen berget ihr im düst'ren Schrein
und führt ihr trauernd daher?

ZWEITER ZUG

Es birgt den Helden der Trauerschrein,
er birgt die heilige Kraft,
der Gott selbst einst zur Pflege sich
  gab:
Titurel führen wir her.

ERSTER ZUG

Wer hat ihn gefällt, der in Gottes Hut,
Gott selbst einst beschirmte?

ZWEITER ZUG

Ihn fällte des Alters tötende Last,
da den Gral er nicht mehr erschaute.

ERSTER ZUG

Wer wehrt' ihm des Grales Huld zu
  erschauen?

ZWEITER ZUG

Den dort ihr geleitet, der sündige
  Hüter.

ERSTER ZUG

Wir geleiten ihn heut', weil heut' noch
  einmal,
zum letzten Male,
will des Amtes er walten.

ZWEITER ZUG

Wehe! Wehe! Du Hüter des Grals!
Zum letzten Male
sei deines Amts gemahnt!

(*Der Sarg ist auf dem Katafalk niedergesetzt, Amfortas auf das Ruhebett
gelegt.*)

AMFORTAS

Ja, Wehe! Wehe! Weh' über mich!
So ruf' ich willig mit euch.
Williger nähm' ich von euch den Tod,
der Sünde mildeste Sühne!

(*Der Sarg ist geöffnet worden. Beim
Anblick der Leiche Titurel's bricht
Alles in einen jähen Wehruf aus.*)

AMFORTAS

(*vom seinem Lager sich hoch aufrich-
tend*)

Mein Vater!
Hochgesegneter der Helden!

His gentle, loving care, and for him
  died,
so man this day reflects His love and
  walks with gentle stride.
All creatures now show gratitude,
—which bloom a spell and then pass
  hence,—
that smiling Nature is renewed
in this sweet day of innocence.

(*Kundry has again slowly lifted her
  head and now looks with moist eyes
  in serious, quiet appeal.*)

PARSIFAL

One time they jeered me, and now
  they wither.
Do they, too, seek redemption hither?
With blessed dew your gentle eyes are
  filling.
You're crying. Look, the fields are
  smiling!

(*He kisses her gently on the forehead,
  a distant pealing of bells is heard.*)

GURNEMANZ

Midday: the time has come.
Give leave, My Lord, for your servant
  to lead you.

(*Gurnemanz brings out his mantle as
  knight of the Grail, and with Kundry's help places it upon Parsifal,
  who, solemnly taking up his lance,
  slowly follows Gurnemanz with Kundry. The scene gradually changes to
  a landscape like that of the first act.
  After a time the three are lost to
  sight as the forest changes into a
  vaulted, rocky passage. The sound
  of bells continually increases in the
  rocky passages.*)

*Finally the scene opens into the great
  hall of the Grail Temple as in the
  first act, save that the refection tables
  are missing. From one side approach
  knights of the Grail bearing Titurel
  in his coffin; from the other a similar*

*train escorting Amfortas on his litter,
  preceded by the Grail.*)

FIRST PROCESSION
We slowly bear in sheltering shrine
the Grail to holiest service.
What lies within your gloomy shrine?
What's brought with sorrowing steps?
(*The two processions march past each
  other.*)

SECOND PROCESSION
The hero lies in the fun'ral shrine.
It hides the heavenly power
which God Himself once gave to His
  charge.
Titurel lies in this bier.

FIRST PROCESSION
What happened to him, who with lov-
  ing care
God Himself protected?

SECOND PROCESSION
He bowed to belief of conquering age
when the sight of the Grail was denied
  him.

FIRST PROCESSION
Who was it withheld the grace of the
  Grail?

SECOND PROCESSION
The one you are bearing, both guardian
  and sinner.

FIRST PROCESSION
We must bear him today, just one
  time longer.
This last time only let him carry the
  office.
Ah, the final time! Sorrow!
Guardian of the Grail, the final time
  let him carry the office.

SECOND PROCESSION
Sorrow, O guardian of the Grail.
Ah, this final time. Now let the rite
  be performed.
This final time let him carry the office.

AMFORTAS
(*wearily raising himself a little*)
Yes, sorrow! Sorrow! Sorrow through
  me.
Yes, all your sorrows are mine.
Gladly would I take my death from
  you,
for sin like mine, that is little.
(*The coffin is opened. At sight of
  Titurel all lament. Amfortas raises
  himself high on his couch and turns
  to Titurel's corpse.*)
My father! Highest blest among all
  heroes!

Du Reinster, dem einst die Engel sich
    neigten!
Der einzig ich sterben wollt'
dir gab ich den Tod!
Oh! der du jetzt in göttlichem Glanz
den Erlöser selbst erschau'st,
erflehe von ihm, dass sein heiliges Blut,
wenn noch einmal heut' sein Segen
die Brüder soll erquicken,
wie ihnen neues Leben,
mir endlich spende den Tod!
Tod! Sterben!
Einzige Gnade!
Die schreckliche Wunde, das Gift er-
    sterbe,
das es zernagt, erstarre das Herz!
Mein Vater! Dich ruf' ich,
rufe du ihm es zu:
Erlöser, gib meinem Sohne Ruh'!

DIE RITTER

(*sich näher an Amfortas drängend,
durcheinander*)

Enthüllet den Gral!
Walte des Amtes!
Dich mahnet dein Vater:
du musst, du musst!

AMFORTAS

(*in wütender Verzweiflung aufspring-
end, und unter die zurückweichen-
den Ritter sich stürzend*)

Nein! Nicht mehr! Ha!
Schon fühl' ich den Tod mich um-
    nachten,
und noch einmal sollt' ich in's Leben
    zurück?
Wahnsinnige!
Wer will mich zwingen zu leben?
Könnt ihr doch Tod mir nur geben!

(*Er reisst sich das Gewand auf.*)

Hier bin ich, die off'ne Wunde hier!
Das mich vergiftet, hier fliesst mein
    Blut:
heraus die Waffen! Taucht eure
    Schwerter
tief, tief auf! bis an's Heft!
Ihr Helden,
Tötet den Sünder mit seiner Qual,
von selbst dann leuchtet euch wohl der
    Gral!

(*Alle sind scheu vor ihm gewichen.
Amfortas steht, in furchtbarer Ex-
tase, einsam.—Parsifal ist von Gur-*

nemanz und Kundry begleitet, unvermerkt unter den Rittern erschien-
en, tritt jetzt hervor, und streckt den
Speer aus, mit dessen Spitze er Amfortas' Seite berührt.)

PARSIFAL

Nur eine Waffe taugt:
die Wunde schliesst
der Speer nur, der sie schlug.

(*Amfortas' Miene leuchtet in Heiliger
Entzückung auf; er scheint vor grosser Ergriffenheit zu schwanken; Gurnemanz stützt ihn.*)

Sei heil, entsündigt und entsühnt!
Denn ich verwalte nun dein Amt.
Gesegnet sei dein Leiden,
das Mitleid's höchste Kraft,
und reinsten Wissens Macht
dem zagen Toren gab.
Den heil'gen Speer,
ich bring' ihn euch zurück!

(*Alles blickt in höchster Entzückung
auf den emporgehaltenen Speer, zu
dessen Spitze aufschauend Parsifal
in Begeisterung fortfährt.*)

Oh! Welchen Wunders höchtes Glück!
Die deine Wunde durfte schliessen,
ihm seh' ich heil'ges Blut entfliessen
in Sehnsucht dem verwandten Quelle,
der dort fliesst in des Grales Welle.
Nicht soll der mehr verschlossen sein:
Enthüllt den Gral! Oeffnet den
    Schrein!

(*Die Knappen öffnen den Schrein:
Parsifal entnimmt diesem den
"Gral", und versenkt sich, unter stum-
men Gebete, in seinen Anblick.
Der "Gral" erglüht; eine Glorienbe-
leuchtung ergiesst sich über Alle.—
Titurel, für diesen Augenblick wieder
belebt, erhebt sich segnend im Sarge.
—Aus der Kuppel schwebt eine weis-
se Taube herab und verweilt über
Parsifal's Haupte. Dieser schwenkt
den "Gral" sanft vor der aufblicken-
den Ritterschaft.—Kundry sinkt, mit
dem Blicke zu ihm auf, langsam
vor Parsifal entseelt zu Boden. Amfortas und Gurnemanz huldigen
kniend Parsifal.*)

ALLE

Höchsten Heiles Wunder!
Erlösung dem Erlöser!

ENDE DER OPER

The purest,
obeyed once even by angels!
For whom I would give my life!
To you I brought death!
Oh, you who now in heavenly rapture
  do gaze upon our Lord,
implore Him for me, that His holiest
  blood
(if but once more now His blessing
may quicken all the brothers,
renewing life within them)
may fin'lly bring me to death!
Death—only, only mercy!
These terrible tortures, their sting, this
  poison!
Oh let it end! Crush life from my
heart!
O Father, I call you!
Ask for help. Plead for me:
"Redeemer, grant to my son relief!"

(*The knights press nearer to Amfortas.*)

THE KNIGHTS

Uncover the Grail!
Serve now your office!
Your father commands you:
You must! you must!

AMFORTAS

(*springs up in raging despair and
rushes into the midst of his knights*)

No more! Ha!
Death comes, for I feel him approach-
  ing!
And yet you would summon me back
  to life?
Insanity!
Who would enforce me to live now,
when death is all I am seeking?

  (*He tears open his garment.*)

Here am I! My open wound is here!
Here is the poison! Here flows my
  blood!
Out with your weapons!
Bury your swords here, deep, deep—
  to the hilt!
Up! You heroes!
Slay both at once: sinner and his sin.
Perhaps the Grail will shine then for
  you!

(*The knights have all fallen back in
fear, leaving Amfortas standing alone
in horrible ecstasy. Parsifal, accom-*

*panied by Gurnemanz and Kundry,
has appeared unnoticed. He now
steps forward and with the point of
the lance touches the side of Amfortas.*)

PARSIFAL

One weapon only serves:
only the spear which gave the wound
  heals the wound.

(*The features of Amfortas light up as
with sacred rapture. He staggers and
is supported by Gurnemanz.*)

Be whole, forgiven, and absolved!
For I must now perform your charge!
And blessed be your suff'ring,
which gave the power of love
and strength of purity to him—
the timid fool!
The sacred spear—I bring it back to
  you!

(*All gaze in the highest exaltation upon the spear, while Parsifal, looking
upon the point, continues in a tone
of exaltation.*)

Oh! Wondrous joy beyond compare!
The spear that touched the wound and
  healed it
is flowing now with blood most holy
which seeks to rejoin its kindred fountain
that wells within the holy vessel.
Nevermore let the cup be hid!
Uncover the Grail! Open the shrine!

(*Parsifal ascends the altar steps, takes
the Grail from the shrine, which has
been opened by the esquires, and
kneels before it in silent prayer. The
Grail gradually glows with a soft
light. The darkness increases from
below, and the illumination from
above.*)

CHORUS

Highest healing's wonder!
Salvation to the Saviour!

(*A ray of light falls: the Grail's glow
is at its brightest. A white dove
descends from the dome and hovers
over Parsifal's head. Kundry, eyes
uplifted to Parsifal, slowly sinks lifeless to the ground before him. Amfortas and Gurnemanz kneel in
homage before Parsifal, who waves
the Grail in blessing over the wor-
shiping Templars.*)

THE END